# JOHANN SEBASTIAN BACH

# SONATAS AND PARTITAS
## SONATEN UND PARTITEN

für Violin solo / for Violine solo

BWV 1001–1006

Transcribed for Viola by
Übertragung für Viola von

Simon Roland-Jones

Editorial Consultant / Wissenschaftlicher Mitarbeiter

David Ledbetter

ALLE RECHTE VORBEHALTEN · ALL RIGHTS RESERVED

**EDITION PETERS**
Leipzig · London · New York

© 2017 by Peters Edition Ltd, London

Alle Rechte vorbehalten · All rights reserved
Vervielfältigungen jeglicher Art sind gesetzlich verboten.
Any unauthorized reproduction is prohibited by law.

ISMN 979-0-57701-104-2

# Contents / Inhalt

Preface / Vorwort ............................................................................................. VI / XI
    The nature of the collection / Die Beschaffenheit der Sammlung ............................ VI / XI
    Sources / Quellen ............................................................................................. VI / XII
    Critical Commentary / Kritischer Bericht ........................................................... VI / XII
    Transcription and the viola / Die Transkription für Viola ................................... VII / XII
    Slurs and bowing / Legatobögen und Bogenführung ......................................... VII / XII
        The Adagio of Sonata I / Das Adagio in Sonate I ........................................ VII / XII
        General points / Allgemeine Bemerkungen .............................................. VIII / XIII
        Counterpoint / Kontrapunkt .................................................................... VIII / XIV
    Ornaments / Verzierungen ............................................................................ VIII / XIV
    Other notations / Andere Notationsformen ..................................................... IX / XV
    Mixed Style / Gemischter Stil ......................................................................... IX / XV

\*\*\*

Sonata 1   C minor / c-Moll (BWV 1001) ..................................................................... 1
Partita 1   E minor / e-Moll (BWV 1002) ...................................................................... 8
Sonata 2   D minor / d-Moll (BWV 1003) ................................................................... 18
Partita 2   G minor / g-Moll (BWV 1004) ................................................................... 28
Sonata 3   F major / F-Dur (BWV 1005) ..................................................................... 40
Partita 3   A major / A-Dur (BWV 1006) .................................................................... 52

\*\*\*

Critical Commentary ............................................................................................ 62
Appendix ............................................................................................................. 64
References ........................................................................................................... 67

JOHANN SEBASTIAN BACH

*Adagio* from Sonata I G minor BWV 1001 in Bach's autograph fair copy

(Staatsbibliothek zu Berlin. Preußischer Kulturbesitz. Shelfmark Mus. ms Bach P 967)

*Reproduced with kind permission of the Music Department and Mendelssohn Archive at the Staatsbibliothek zu Berlin. Preußischer Kulturbesitz · bpk-Bildagentur*

In his carefully prepared fair copy of the Solos Bach's expressive handwriting
appears to suggest the way he felt his music as he wrote it down.
The *Adagio* of Sonata I is one of the most complex movements and its notation
demonstrates many of Bach's writing habits, particularly his use of performance indications.
The need to understand and interpret these is discussed in the Preface and Critical Commentary.

*Adagio* aus der Sonate Nr. I g-Moll BWV 1001 in Bachs autographer Reinschrift

(Staatsbibliothek zu Berlin. Preußischer Kulturbesitz. Signatur Mus. ms Bach P 967)

*Abdruck mit freundlicher Genehmigung der Staatsbibliothek zu Berlin. Preußischer Kulturbesitz. Musikabteilung mit Mendelssohn-Archiv · bpk-Bildagentur*

Bachs ausdrucksstarker Schrift im Autograph der Solostücke ist geradezu anzusehen,
wie sich der Gefühlsgehalt der Musik bei der Notation niederschlug.
Das *Adagio* der ersten Sonate ist einer der komplexesten Sätze der Sammlung und zeigt exemplarisch
viele Schreibgewohnheiten Bachs, besonders hinsichtlich der Verwendung von Vortragsbezeichnungen.
Auf die Wichtigkeit eines korrekten Lesens und Verstehens dieser Eigenheiten
wird im Vorwort sowie im Kritischen Bericht eingegangen.

JOHANN SEBASTIAN BACH

*Adagio* from Sonata I G minor BWV 1001 in Bach's autograph fair copy

*Adagio* aus Sonate I g-Moll BWV 1001 in Bachs autographer Reinschrift

# Preface

Bach's Sonatas and Partitas for Solo Violin have been regarded as a pinnacle of the violin repertory virtually ever since they were composed. Starting with Bach's circle of friends and pupils, their fame spread during the eighteenth century with advocacy from prominent virtuosos such as Jean-Baptiste Cartier in Paris and Johann Peter Salomon in London. During the nineteenth century they were introduced to a larger concert public by Joseph Joachim. Now they are regarded as everything that a set of works is capable of being: superb concert repertory, superb material for students to work at, and, not least, superb examples of compositional techniques. Yet even in Bach's own time people commented that, despite its complexity, Bach's music speaks to humanity as a whole, profoundly, and regardless of whether or not listeners have any musical training. The aim of this edition is to encourage viola players to become more familiar with these great works, and at the same time help them interpret Bach's ambiguous performance markings as a string player of the period might have done.

## *The nature of the collection*

Bach's own title for the set was *Sei Solo ã Violino senza Baßo accompagnato* (Six Solos for violin without accompanying bass); the usual modern title dates from the edition by Joseph Joachim and Andreas Moser (Berlin, 1908).[1] Bach dated the title-page of the fair-copy autograph manuscript 1720, the year in which his first wife, Maria Barbara, died, and some have romantically seen the Solos as a memorial to her (the Italian title, with *Solo* not *Soli*, can be read as 'You are alone'). It could equally be Bach warning the violinist 'You are on your own', or more likely Bach using a title along the lines of the *Six Trio* (not *Trios*) published by his friend and colleague Telemann in 1718. In 1720 Bach reached the age of thirty-five, half way through the Biblical life-span of seventy years. A devout Lutheran, he began in that year a series of collections of compositions of different types that may be considered summations of his philosophy of music as it had developed. They are remarkable for their comprehensiveness and for what one might call the specific gravity of the music. The Brandenburg Concertos arrived in 1721, the first Well-tempered Clavier in 1722, and so on until The Art of Fugue and the B minor Mass in his final years. It says much for the importance to him of the instrument that the very first of these collections should have been for violin.

Within a concise framework, the Six Solos cover all the types of composition that Bach was to demonstrate in a series of keyboard collections over the following years. Each Sonata begins with the equivalent of a prelude and fugue. Within that, the Fuga of Sonata I has a canzona-type subject, Sonata II a dance type, and Sonata III a mannered *stile antico* type. The fugues of Sonatas II and III have falling semitones in their countersubjects. This is not necessarily an expressive lament motif, it can also be a mannered or learned feature. It was a common element in polyphonic music for violin or bass viol on account of its convenience for invertible counterpoint in double stopping. In Sonata III it provides mannered chromaticism as a foil for the diatonic subject. In addition to comprehensiveness of styles, each successive fugue is on a more complex formal plan. The Fuga in Sonata I is in the manner of a concerto, with equivalents of tutti ritornellos and solo episodes; Sonata II adds to this a binary element suitable for its dance style; and Sonata III combines concerto and binary elements with a da capo. The systematic increase of formal complexity suggests that this was also the order in which the pieces were composed. The third movements also cover a range of violin genres. Sonata I is in the manner of a trio, in dance rhythm; Sonata 2 the slow movement of a Venetian concerto, with soft repeated chords in the upper strings supporting a florid solo melody; Sonata 3 a sonata for violin and continuo.

The Partitas equally present a comprehensive range of types.[2] Partitas I and II represent different techniques of variation. Each movement of Partita I has a Double (a French term for what in English is called a division variation, dividing the piece into smaller note values). Again there is a comprehensive range: the Tempo di Borea Double has eighth notes, the Sarabande triplets, the Allemanda and Corrente sixteenths. Partita II represents a different, traditionally German, variation type with each movement developed from a common harmonic template at the opening. Harmonic formulas used in the first four movements are then resumed in the most comprehensive movement of all, the Ciaccona. In itself a variation form, the Ciaccona ranges from the metre of a French chaconne, to the measured liveliness of Corelli, the eccentric virtuosity of Vivaldi and the extravagant brilliance of Biber. Partita III has a different agenda, of exploring the mixed style of Bach's generation. It starts with a purely Italianate Preludio, followed by a purely French Loure. The two styles are then mixed together in various ways until the final Gigue returns to the Italian style. Along the way a range of formal possibilities is again demonstrated, in a Gavotte en rondeaux, *alternativement* Menuets, and a plain binary Bourée.

## *Sources*

The three principal sources used for this edition are: Bach's autograph fair copy, dated 1720 (Source **A**); a copy made by Anna Magdalena Bach (Source **B**); and a copy made in the Bach circle in the early 1720s (Source **C**). For further information see the Sources list in the **Critical Commentary**.

## *Critical Commentary*

The **Critical Commentary** identifies problems in interpreting Source **A**. Where relevant the **Commentary** compares readings from Sources **B** and **C** and explains the reasons for editorial decisions. Often several solutions may be possible and players are strongly advised to use the **Commentary** in forming their own interpretations. It is an essential complement to the following comments on interpreting the autograph. The main criterion for decisions should always be what best supports the expressive projection of the music.

Editorial bowings that relate to preceding or analogous passages are marked as editorial in the score (with a dotted slur) but not necessarily listed in the **Commentary**. Where there are many occurrences of the same pattern within one movement the suggestion is given only on the first appearance (for example, **Sonata I, Fuga** bar 1; **Siciliana** bar 1, and see below *General points*).

---

[1] *Sonaten und Partiten für Violine allein.*

[2] Bach's title is Partia, a traditional German title for a suite.

## Transcription and the viola

The present transcription transposes the Solos down one fifth without further alteration. Pitches are always referred to as the pitches in the transposed viola version, even when referring to the sources. Although there is one supremely authoritative source for the Solos, editing it is not as straightforward as might at first seem. There are numerous ambiguities in the performance indications that have to be interpreted. This is particularly so with slurs, in their often unclear placement and also in that, although many of the slurs are practical bowing instructions, some have a more analytical function of showing harmonic or contrapuntal progressions. The aim of this edition is to provide viola players with a usable performing score that respects the original as much as possible but does not shirk from interpreting the notation where necessary, in the light of Baroque performing practice and the practicalities of the viola.

It would be a pity if players were to limit themselves to the easier movements, put off from further exploration by technical difficulties that are less problematic on the violin. Passages in two or more parts can at times seem almost unplayable on the viola if taken literally and players need to exercise some ingenuity. For an example of a suggested solution to a passage of this sort see **Appendix** Example 3.

Chords can be a problem on the viola, especially three- and four-part ones, in that they can easily become heavy and aggressive. It may therefore be a good idea to think of them as generally well arpeggiated. For chords, as well as for the all-important right-hand expression, the use of a Baroque bow is well worth considering. However, if using a modern bow, a lighter Baroque-bow feeling may be at least partially simulated by holding the bow further up, just past the thumb-pad. It is worth remembering that in polyphonic passages there is usually a single leading line, and primary attention should be concentrated on shaping that. The rest can then be fitted around it. It is thought that Baroque string players were adept at hinting at polyphony by spreading chords and by dynamic nuance.

The consensus of historically informed players today is that chords that have the leading voice in the bass should be played the same way as other chords, i.e. from the bass note up rather than from the top downwards (for example **Sonata I, Siciliana** bar 4 third beat).[3] Given the impossibility of playing the first beat of bar 5 upside down (and many similar places) because of the moving upper parts, it is unlikely that the third beat of bar 4 or the first beat of bar 19 were intended to be spread downwards.[4]

Lastly, it is perhaps a good idea to keep in mind that big stretches, even greater on the viola, are often easier to manage without vibrato, although vibrato in itself is of course a vital part of an appropriately nuanced expression.[5]

---

[3] In $\frac{12}{8}$ metre one beat refers to a ♩. note.

[4] For ways of spreading chords in Bach's time see Boyden, 1965, pp. 435–8.

[5] For a full discussion of vibrato in the Baroque period see Moens-Haenen, 1988.

# Slurs and bowing

## The Adagio of Sonata I

Slurs and bowing account for by far the majority of problems in interpreting Bach's notation. Most types of problem are present in the Adagio of Sonata I (see the frontispiece). They begin in bar 1: the slur in the second beat is obviously too short and should cover the whole group to the end of the beat. In spite of Bach's exceptional care in notating performance indications in the Solos, the point at which slurs should begin and end is not infrequently ambiguous and it requires experience of Bach's writing habits and the conventions of Baroque bowing to interpret them. A good background principle for the Adagio, where some slurs may seem ambiguous and illogical, is to try one bow per beat.

Next, there is a slur missing from the 7–6 appoggiatura in the third beat. Bach by no means wrote in every single slur he intended and left much to the player. The appoggiatura is part of the thematic material of the piece and every other instance of it has a slur. Slurring appoggiaturas to their resolutions was a performance convention, taken for granted along with slurring trills to their termination and so on (see also the first beat of bar 10). Generally speaking, Bach's policy was to notate essentials and leave more conventional matters to performers.

The slur in the first half of bar 2 is a problem as a bowing slur since, if it begins on the tied note, it will not only result in an extremely long bow but also give an undesirable up-bow on the third-beat chord. It is therefore probably best interpreted as an analytical slur showing that the first half of the bar is all a decorated resolution of the 7th ($f'$) in the first beat to $eb'$ in the third beat. Whatever bowing is adopted should support that effect. The very florid decoration in the second half of bar 3 ornaments the 7th ($g'$) resolving to $f'$ in the trill at the end of the bar. In this case the slur needs to begin on the tied note; Bach wrote it slightly to the right presumably to avoid an untidy clash with the flat sign.

A similar case where Bach's writing habits need to be taken into account is in the third beat of bar 4. Bach liked to keep everything within the stave and disliked writing slurs that clash with accidentals or note stems and flags. When there is a chord at the beginning of a beat he therefore tends to write the slur to the right. There are many instances. In this case editors have given the slur variously, either literally as 1 + 3, or interpreted it as 3 + 1. Another good background principle is to imagine the passage without the chord and ask what bowing would best project the leading line in the bar as a whole (see also bar 5 third beat and bar 17 third beat; also **Fuga** bar 12 first beat, bar 57 fourth beat; other cases are **Sonata II, Grave** bar 7 third beat; **Partita I, Sarabande** bar 5 third beat; **Partita II, Sarabande** bar 7 third beat; **Ciaccona** bars 4, 5, 252, 253).

A retake can be important for dramatic effect. From the beginning of bar 20 the line progresses up from the bottom string to the emphatic 5/4 chord on the third beat of bar 21, which has the climaxing effect of a cadenza point. Successive down-bows can yield a wide range of articulations, from this dramatic accent to **Partita III, Gavotte en rondeaux** bar 6, which seems to ask for the slight gap produced by a retake, whereas the half note in bar 2 demands a more through feeling.

## General points

Players may wish to slur notes that are not slurred in the sources, for example when eighths and quarter notes are combined in two parts. Generally slurs suit small intervals such as 2nds and 3rds, but seem less likely over wider intervals (for example **Partita I, Sarabande** bar 3, where the second and third beats could well be slurred, though probably not the first beat).

Slurs combined with the triplet marking *3* (for example **Partitas I and II, Allemanda**) need not necessarily be regarded as bowing. Patterns may be varied, as suggested by Leopold Mozart in Chapter VI of his *Violinschule*.[6] Unslurred triplets might also have varied bowings, as in **Partita I, Sarabande Double** (the marks at strain-ends in the autograph, known as *chapeaux*, are to indicate first-time bars).

The slur to indicate the tied trill (see *Ornaments*) is conventional and may lead to awkward bowing. Editorial bowings are suggested to address this problem (**Partita I, Allemanda** bar 7 fourth beat etc., **Sonata II, Grave** bar 2 second beat etc.).

In **Sonata I, Siciliana**, the down-up-down-up-up bowing works well at the beginning (as editorially suggested), but in the sequence at bars 9ff a down-up-up-down-up pattern may be preferable, creating a greater sense of direction.

Fugue subjects need careful consideration. In **Sonata I, Fuga**, two up-bows for the pair of sixteenths in the subject is possible but seems rather too light for the serious, canzona style: therefore the editorial bowing down-down-up is suggested. However, when the texture builds up, at bar 3 etc., down-up-up may help the chords to speak better. In **Sonata II, Fuga,** the down-up-down that is the natural way to bow the beginning could continue to work well throughout the remainder of the movement. In **Sonata III, Fuga**, the suggested bowing for the subject, best accomplished with virtually no retakes on the successive down-bows, produces a calmer and more orderly effect than bowing it out, opening the way for a very long fugue. As the texture builds, the same bowing will not necessarily work and other solutions will need to be found by any player who is resourceful enough to tackle this *tour de force*. In the rocking pedal passages from bar 186 etc., changing bow every eighth note, rather than every quarter, produces greater resonance.

In the many cases in **Partita I, Allemanda**, where a dotted note is followed by two 32nds a variety of bowing is possible depending on the desired effect. Georg Muffat suggests either bowing all separately, or 'for greater sweetness' bowing both short notes in with the dotted note, or bowing just the two short notes as a pair 'as seems appropriate'.[7]

Some slurs are better regarded as analytical phrasing marks rather than bowing indications, as in the example from **Sonata I, Adagio** bar 2, mentioned above. Another example is in **Sonata III, Largo** bar 19, where the long slur may imply a fading away rather than necessarily a bowing.

## Counterpoint

Bach's notation of counterpoint for solo stringed instruments tends to present an ideal contrapuntal texture rather than something that has to be played exactly as written, a fact not understood by advocates of the old Vega 'Bach bow' which was designed to allow the violin to sound like an organ. The art is to convey the effect of the counterpoint convincingly. For example, there are many places where shorter notes are combined with longer notes. In such instances the shorter notes may need to be slurred, as indicated in **Sonata I, Fuga** bars 15–18 (**Appendix** Example 1) and **Sonata III, Fuga** bars 115–21 (**Appendix** Example 6), but slurs could also be an alternative to separate bows for much of **Sonata II, Andante** (**Appendix** Example 4). Cutting the tied note would help alleviate the very awkward stretch (on the viola) in **Sonata II, Fuga** bars 128–30 (**Appendix** Example 3). In **Sonata III, Fuga** bars 161–2, the lower two parts will need to be bowed separately and so there is no possibility of sustaining the top note.

In **Sonata III, Adagio**, the bowing of one bow per beat could be continued where practical throughout the movement. At bars 34–6 the long notes in the upper part again could be held for less than their entire length. This piece is a good example of the need to vary bowings according to the taste of the player.

The notes of the chromatic countersubject of **Sonata III, Fuga** bars 4ff, need to be slightly separated, not slurred, and all the same length. The same applies to **Sonata II, Fuga** bars 5ff.

## Ornaments

There are many introductions to Baroque ornamentation.[8] Bach wrote a brief explanation of his usual ornament signs in the *Clavier-Büchlein* for Wilhelm Friedemann Bach (see **Appendix** Example 8). It is a table of thirteen ornaments and dates from 1720, the same year as the autograph of the Solos. However, Bach seems to have regarded the Solos as a neutral reference copy and used only one ornament sign (*tr* for a trill), leaving other essential ornaments to the player.[9] The more complex ornaments he wrote out in notes, part of the care he took over the notation of the Solos. In building an interpretation of the floridly decorated slow movements it is worth considering Bach's 1720 ornament table since imagining the ornament sign behind the notes can help to give the necessary freedom in shaping decorative groups.

Trills generally begin with an accented upper note, but there are many cases where the ornamented note is approached by step from above, with a slur, giving a tied trill. Trills are commonly tied in descending steps in a decorative (i.e. short) note value, where it is better not to repeat the upper note as this would break the line. A typical situation is **Sonata III, Largo** bar 6 third beat; later (bars 16f) Bach has written in the implied slur. Another case is in **Partita I, Allemanda** bar 2 second beat, where the *g′* could be slurred to the *f♯′* and the trill consist of only three notes (for the character of this piece see *Mixed style* below).

---

[6] Mozart 1756. This tutor should not be thought of as too late for this repertory. It was published only four years after Quantz's *Versuch* and was based on earlier publications of Tartini. It deals predominantly with Italian style, whereas Quantz also has a great deal to say about French-style performance.

[7] Muffat 1698, see Wilson 2001, p. 40; Kolneder 1990, pp. 64–7.

[8] The subject is not without controversy. Good concise introductions to Bach's ornaments are Emery 1953 and Klotz 1984. Both have reproductions of Bach's table of 1720; Klotz gives many more tables from Bach's environment.

[9] The lack of essential ornament signs is notable in comparison with Bach's autograph 'lute' arrangement of Partita III (BWV 1006a), see *Mixed styles* below.

Two ornamental patterns that occur many times in the Solos are in the second and third beats of **Sonata II, Grave** bar 2. The first, in beat two, is essentially a compound ornament combining an appoggiatura, trill and mordent. In quick note values such as the 32nds here the trill may be of only three notes, the upper note *e′* notionally tied to the eighth-note appoggiatura (see Example). This is a delicate ornament, with an accented appoggiatura and the rest of the beat fading away.

The second pattern, in beat three, has a simple trill, but this time the approach to it, from *d′* to *c′*, is into a beat and from a short note to a longer one so the *d′* should be repeated (the pattern in this beat is a version of the *coulé de tierce*, see *Other notations*).

Appoggiaturas should be leant on (*appoggiare/appuyer* = to lean on), slurred to the resolution and the resolution note lightened. In **Partita III, Loure** bar 6 etc., appoggiaturas take the weight off the main note. Trills on resolution notes therefore need to be very light, as in **Sonata I, Adagio** bar 4 first beat.

For the cadential trill François Couperin gives a generally useful prescription. It has three ingredients: (a) the appoggiatura (*appuy*), which should be accented; (b) the repetitions, which should start in a leisurely way and get quicker; and (c) the stopping point (*point d'arrêt*), which should coincide with the second bass eighth (i.e. stop on the dot). The anticipation of the final tonic note (d) should be played short.[10]

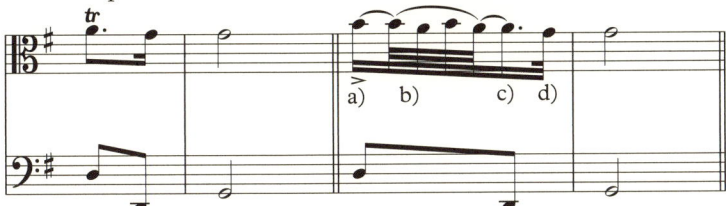

Bach has notated a tied version of this in **Sonata III, Adagio** bar 14. A trill sign on the *d′* in this situation is one of those conventional things that Bach did not always bother notating. Here the appoggiatura *eb′* is tied to the first note of the trill.

## Other notations

Quarter barlines in triple time were commonly used by Bach up to the mid-1720s. In **Sonata I, Presto**, they give a more vigorous effect than would §-time and emphasize the cross-rhythms. In **Partita I, Corrente**, they again give the effect of on-bars and off-bars, expressed in alternating bowing patterns.

The prolongation dot in this music has not only the effect of lengthening a note but can also imply an accent.[11] This explains why the one place in **Partita II, Corrente**, where the quarter note has a dot is the chord in bar 49. It is a climax point that has been built up to, and the dot implies an accent and a slight fermata. Accented dotted notes are particularly associated with tiratas. In **Sonata II, Grave** bar 1 fourth beat, the tirata is introduced as part of the motivic network of the piece. In bar 5 it is developed into a triple tirata, building to the climax in bar 6. The dot signifies an accent and slight pause, rather than an exact value, so there is a four-note tirata, then a six-note tirata, then a more regular final ornament. Editors tend to change Bach's notation here, and particularly to omit the dot on the *a′*. Although Bach's beaming for the third and fourth beats is not quite accurate, his notation succeeds in conveying a vital expressive nuance.

The wavy lines at the end of **Sonata II, Grave**, have been interpreted in various ways.[12] The most likely solution seems to be a subtle ondeggiando, a rapid rocking effect on the double stop, alternating the weight of the bow between the two notes without losing either note. The wavy lines stop on the second quarter note, when the ondeggiando turns into a trill in the upper part. The aim should be to heighten the rhetorical effect of the Phrygian cadence that prepares the **Fuga**, which should begin immediately (there is no fermata), the subject picking up the octave dominant and bringing it to the tonic in bar 2.

**Sonata I, Adagio**, ends with a perfect cadence and a fermata on the final chord, so there can be a slight pause before the Fuga. The **first movements of Sonatas II and III** both end with an imperfect cadence. There is no fermata and Bach has written the time signature of the Fuga on the last line, immediately after the double bar, as a kind of direct implying that the player goes straight into the Fuga.

## Mixed Style

The German lands were a melting-pot of musical styles in the later 17th century. The many courts seeking to keep up with fashion employed French and Italian, as well as German, musicians. The most advanced court musically in Bach's environment was at Dresden, among whose many musicians were a French orchestra led by J. B. Volumier, a leading Italian virtuoso violinist in F. M. Veracini, and an advanced and sophisticated German connoisseur of styles in J. G. Pisendel. Part of the aim of the Solos is to represent the German mixed style which drew on the two main styles, French and Italian, and also on Polish and even English elements.[13]

Each of the Solos presents some version of mixed style and this variety is part of their nature as a compendium for connoisseurs of musical styles and techniques. The **Fuga of Sonata II**, for example, treats a light French dance metre (bourrée) with fugal technique, in an Italian concerto format with concertante figurations, bariolage, and even echoes, a mixture very characteristic of Bach.

All three Partitas are notable demonstrations of different styles. The **Allemanda** of **Partita I** confronts the metrical style of a sophisticated French allemande with the Italian sonata style of continuous sixteenths in its Double, as it were François Couperin opposed to Corelli.[14] It is important to understand this since the wide leaps and dotted rhythm of the Allemanda can look like an aggressively jagged and dissonant line. Approached from the French tradition it is clearly a piece in *style brisé*

---

[10] Couperin 1717, p. 24.

[11] See Quantz 1752, XVII vii §56, 58.

[12] For a survey of possible interpretations see Ledbetter 2009, pp. 121–22; also Moens-Haenen 1984.

[13] For Bach's comment on Dresden musicians see *NBR* p. 150; for a detailed explanation of the main elements of mixed style see Ledbetter 2009, Chapter Two.

[14] For a full discussion of the stylistic background see the commentary on this piece in Ledbetter 2009.

(arpeggiated counterpoint with two parts in one) with written-out *notes inégales*. A typical French allemande has the time signature ₵ and the sixteenths are played unequally. Quite how unequally is a matter of taste, depending on the particular stylistic mixture of the piece and the expressive moment. *Notes inégales* are best regarded as an expressive resource, ranging from quite sharply dotted to more like a gentle triplet. When approached from the French lute tradition, with which unaccompanied Baroque string music has much in common, this stylistic character is obvious.[15] Into it Bach has added galant-style triplets. An intricate variety of decorative note values was one feature of the oncoming galant style around 1720.

**Partita I** is in itself a compendium of note values and time relations. The ₵ time signature of the Allemanda Double implies twice the speed of the Allemanda C (♩ = ♪). The Corrente, already in Italian sonata style with a single division note value (eighths) throughout, shares the same 3/4 time signature and tempo with its Double. The Sarabande and its triplet Double should share roughly the same tempo although here the Double invites a more flowing tempo. The Sarabande itself is unusual for its lack of second-beat accents, except at strain ends. This is the point of the slurs over three eighths (bar 10 etc.), the rhythmic equivalent of the dotted quarter note (bar 2 etc.). The prevailing metre of three equal quarter notes with a feeling of upbeat to a dotted quarter gives the cortège-like character of this piece. Standard French inequality in the eighths would be quite inappropriate, but a noticeable strong–weak / on-beat–off-beat pairing of stress helps the character. The Tempo di Borea shares the same character with its Double. Here the division note value (eighths) becomes gradually more prominent in the second strain until it takes over entirely in the Double.

**Partita III** offers another confrontation of styles. The **Preludio** is completely Italian, the **Loure** completely French, with correspondingly different bowing styles. Italians tended to bow things out, French to lift the bow more and have a down-bow at the beginning of the bar.[16] A French writer of the time well described the difference: the French play 'with lifted bow-strokes, all in the air', whereas Italians use 'smooth and well-connected up-bows and down-bows whose changes are imperceptible, producing an endless chain of notes that appear as a continuous flow'.[17] The succeeding dances gradually become more Italianate. The **Gavotte** has a common stylistic mixture, alternating antecedent phrases in dance rhythm with consequent phrases in a division value. The *couplets* range from musette, to sonata, to concertante styles. **Menuet I** starts in dance metre but moves to the sonata style of continuous eighths in its second strain. **Menuet II** alternates rustic musette with elegant sonata styles. The **Bourée** moves further in the direction of continuous eighths, including concertante echoes as in the Preludio, and the **Gigue** completes the return to Italian style.

An important aspect of *notes inégales* is the interpretation of dotted rhythms, such as in **Sonata I, Siciliana** bar 1 first beat, and more so in **Partita III, Loure** bar 1 first beat. Played as written this rhythm lacks poise, a slight inequality is essential to the dance character. Generally it is best to think of a compound-, rather than duple-, time background, for example the first half-bar of the Loure as in 9/8-time, the eighth note coinciding with the last of a triplet. The aim is to have a graceful lilt, without any heaviness or squareness. A particular problem is presented by the opening of the **Ciaccona in Partita II**. Some old performances repeated the chord on the eighth note of bar 1 giving a very heavy, dragging effect. Something of the lilt of a French Chaconne is essential at this stage of the piece, even though the tempo must be considerably slower than a Lully danced chaconne would be. The art is to combine the *allure* of the dance with the grave, not to say tragic, nature of the piece, in a tempo that has to allow it to range subsequently over the main German and Italian virtuoso styles of the time. A further case is where the rhythm does not add up, as with a dotted eighth followed by three 32nds in, for example, **Partita I, Allemanda** bar 5 third beat. Here the speed of the 32nds can match whatever degree of dotting is chosen for this piece.

A very characteristic French punctuation mark is the melodic *coulé de tierce*, commonly used to mark an intermediate phrase ending. It is equivalent of a comma or slight taking of breath by a singer or wind player.[18] Its unadorned form as a falling 3rd is in **Partita III, Loure** bar 1 notes 4–5. In what is perhaps a lute arrangement of this Partita, Bach has written in the usual grace notes (see **Appendix** Example 7): the upper grace note (an appoggiatura/*appuy*) would normally be played on the beat, the other (a *coulé*) played before the lower quarter note and slurred to it.[19] It can take various forms: in bar 4 second half, it is two paired eighths; in **Partita I, Allemanda** bar 5 first beat, it is in lombardic rhythm (short-long), the opposite of the usual (long-short) *notes inégsales*. It is an important articulation point in shaping complex phrases and can also appear among streams of notes in a more Italianate style, as in **Partita II, Allemanda** bar 6 first beat, where it marks the end of the first sentence.

November 2016 *David Ledbetter*

---

[15] Of good lute recordings, Nigel North's early CD was a stylistic revelation to many (Linn Records CKD 013, 1994).

[16] See Georg Muffat 1698 section II in Wilson 2001, especially p. 40; Kolneder 1990, pp. 66–7.

[17] Le Blanc 1740, see Ledbetter 2009, p. 39.

[18] It should be distinguished from the *tierce coulée*, a keyboard ornament, normally a 3rd written as a dyad with a slanting stroke between the notes. This is simply a passing-note addition to an arpeggiated interval or chord and has no significance in melodic punctuation.

[19] For BWV 1006a see the commentary in Ledbetter 2009; it is edited in *NBA* V/10. In Ex. 7 Bach clearly intended the standard French version, with the *coulé* before the lower note, so that the bass can enter on *a* in the last beat.

# Vorwort

Bachs Sonaten und Partiten für Violine solo gelten seit ihrer Entstehung als ein Höhepunkt der Violinliteratur. Über Bachs Freundes- und Schülerkreis hinaus erlangten sie im 18. Jahrhundert Bekanntheit durch prominente Virtuosen wie Jean-Baptiste Cartier in Paris und Johann Peter Salomon in London. Im 19. Jahrhundert wurden sie durch Joseph Joachim einem größeren Konzertpublikum vorgestellt. Heute zeichnen sie sich durch alles aus, was ein Werkkomplex zu sein vermag: großartige Konzertliteratur, vorzügliches Studienmaterial für Schüler und nicht zuletzt Abbilder einer ausgereiften Kompositionstechnik. Bereits zu Bachs Lebzeiten war man der Meinung, dass dessen Musik – trotz ihrer Komplexität – die Menschheit als Ganzes zutiefst anspricht, unabhängig von musikalischer Vorbildung. Das Ziel dieser Ausgabe ist es, Bratschisten zu ermutigen, sich mit diesen wunderbaren Werken vertraut zu machen. Gleichzeitig sollen Hilfen gegeben werden, Bachs mehrdeutige Vortragsbezeichnungen so zu interpretieren, wie es ein Streicher zur damaligen Zeit wohl getan hätte.

## Die Beschaffenheit der Sammlung

Bachs Originaltitel für diese Werke lautete *Sei Solo ã Violino senza Baßo accompagnato* (Sechs Soli für Violine ohne Bass), der heute verwendete Titel geht auf die Ausgabe von Joseph Joachim und Andreas Moser (Berlin, 1908) zurück.[1] Auf der Titelseite der autographen Reinschrift hat Bach das Jahr 1720 vermerkt, das Jahr, in dem seine erste Frau starb. Dies führte mitunter dazu, dass die Soli in das romantische Licht eines musikalischen Denkmals für Maria Barbara Bach gerückt wurden (der italienische Titel, mit *Solo* statt *Soli*, kann als „Du bist allein" gelesen werden). Denkbar ist auch, dass Bach den Geiger mit diesem Titel darauf hinweisen wollte, dass er ganz auf sich selbst gestellt ist. Noch wahrscheinlicher allerdings ist, dass er den Titel analog zu den *Six Trio* (nicht *Trios*) verwendete, die sein Freund und Kollege Telemann 1718 veröffentlicht hatte. 1720 vollendete Bach sein fünfunddreißigstes Lebensjahr – die Halbzeit zum biblischen Alter von siebzig Jahren. Als gläubiger Lutheraner begann Bach in diesem Jahr, eine Reihe von Sammlungen und Stücken verschiedenster Art zu komponieren, die jeweils als Zusammenfassung der von ihm entwickelten Musikphilosophie verstanden werden können. Beeindruckend ist ihre Reichhaltigkeit und ihre besondere Tiefe. Die *Brandenburgischen Konzerte* kamen 1721 hinzu, Teil I des *Wohltemperierten Klaviers* im Jahr 1722 und weitere Werke – bis zur *Kunst der Fuge* und der h-Moll-Messe in seinen letzten Lebensjahren. Die Tatsache, dass Bach die allererste dieser Sammlungen für Violine schrieb, sagt viel über die Bedeutung aus, die das Instrument für ihn hatte.

In einem prägnanten formalen Rahmen zeigen die Sechs Soli alle Kompositionsweisen auf, die Bach in den folgenden Jahren in einer Reihe von Sammlungen für Tasteninstrumente präsentieren wird. Jede der drei Sonaten beginnt mit dem Äquivalent eines Präludiums und einer Fuge. Innerhalb dessen hat die Fuga der ersten Sonate ein Thema nach Art der Kanzone, die der zweiten Sonate ein Thema mit Tanzcharakter und die dritte Sonate ein Thema in der Art eines manieristischen *Stile antico*. Bei den absteigenden Halbtönen innerhalb der Kontrasubjekte der Fugen der Sonaten II und III handelt es sich nicht unbedingt um ein ausdrucksvolles Klagemotiv – es kann auch ein manieristisches oder gelehrtes Merkmal darstellen. In polyphoner Musik für Violine oder Gambe war es aufgrund seiner guten Spielbarkeit im mehrstimmigen Spiel und innerhalb des doppelten Kontrapunkts ein gebräuchliches Element. In der Sonata III bildet die manieristische Chromatik ein Gegenstück zum diatonischen Thema. Über den Stilreichtum hinaus besitzt jede Fuge ein jeweils komplexeres formales Konzept. Die Fuge von Sonata I mit ihren Tutti-Ritornellen und Solopassagen entsprechenden Abschnitten ist im Stil eines Concertos gehalten. In der Sonata II kommt ein dem tänzerischen Charakter entsprechendes zweiteiliges Formelement hinzu, und in der Sonata III sind Konzert- und zweiteilige Formelemente mit einem Da capo kombiniert. Diese systematische Steigerung in der formalen Komplexität legt nahe, dass die Stücke auch in dieser Reihenfolge komponiert wurden. Die dritten Sätze bedienen sich verschiedener Genres der Violinmusik: Der dritte Satz der Sonata I, die einen Tanzrhythmus aufweist, steht im Stil eines Trios, jener der Sonata II im Stil eines langsamen Satzes eines venezianischen Concertos mit leisen wiederholten Akkorden in den hohen Streichern, die eine figurierte Solomelodie stützen, und der dritte Satz der Sonata III steht im Stil einer Sonate für Violine und Basso continuo.

Auch in den Partiten präsentiert Bach eine breite stilistische Palette.[2] In den Partiten I und II werden verschiedene Variationstechniken vorgestellt. Jeder Satz der Partita I hat ein Double (die französische Bezeichnung für eine diminuierende Variation, bei der das Thema in kleineren Notenwerten umspielt wird). Und wieder ist die Palette breit: das Double der Tempo di Borea ist konstituiert durch Achtelnoten, jenes der Sarabanda durch triolische Bildungen, während den Double-Passagen von Allemanda und Corrente Sechzehntel zugrunde liegen. Partita II zeigt eine andere, typisch deutsche Variationsart, bei der sich jeder Satz am Anfang aus einer ähnlichen harmonischen Vorlage bedient. Die in den ersten vier Sätzen verwendeten harmonischen Modelle werden dann in dem längsten aller Sätze, der Ciaccona, wieder aufgenommen. Die Ciaccona, eine Variationsform, erscheint in verschiedenen Ausprägungen, von der Art einer französischen Chaconne über die gemäßigte Lebendigkeit eines Corelli und die exzentrische Virtuosität eines Vivaldi bis hin zur extravaganten Brillanz eines Biber. Partita III ist anderer Herkunft und nimmt den gemischten Stil der Generation Bachs auf. Sie beginnt mit einem italienisch anmutenden Preludio, gefolgt von einer rein französischen Loure. Im weiteren Verlauf kommt es zu einer Vermischung dieser beiden Stile, bis letztendlich die Gigue zum italienischen Stil zurückkehrt. Daneben zeigt sich erneut eine breite Palette formaler Möglichkeiten in einer Gavotte en Rondeaux, *Alternativement*-Menuetten und einer schlichten zweiteiligen Bourée.

---

[1] *Sonaten und Partiten für Violine allein.*

[2] Bachs Titel lautet *Partia*, ein traditionelle deutsche Bezeichnung für eine Suite.

## Quellen

Die drei für diese Ausgabe verwendeten Hauptquellen sind: Bachs autographe Reinschrift, datiert mit 1720 (Quelle **A**), eine von Anna Magdalena Bach angefertigte Abschrift (Quelle **B**) und eine in den frühen 1720er-Jahren im Kreise Bachs entstandene Abschrift (Quelle **C**). Weitere Informationen hierzu finden sich in der Beschreibung der Quellen im **Kritischen Bericht**.

## Kritischer Bericht

Der **Kritische Bericht** zeigt die Schwierigkeiten bei der Interpretation von Quelle **A** auf. Soweit relevant, werden Lesarten aus Quelle **B** und **C** zum Vergleich herangezogen und die Gründe für die Entscheidung des Herausgebers erläutert. Häufig sind mehrere Lösungen möglich, daher wird nachdrücklich empfohlen, den **Kritischen Bericht** zu konsultieren, um zu einer eigenen Interpretation zu gelangen. Der **Kritische Bericht** ist eine unverzichtbare Ergänzung zu den folgenden Kommentaren zur Lesart des Autographs. Das wesentliche Kriterium für editorische Entscheidungen sollte immer sein, was der Musik den besten Ausdruck verleiht.

Vom Herausgeber ergänzte Bindebogen, die einen Bezug zu vorangehenden oder zu analogen Passagen haben, sind in der Partitur als solche gekennzeichnet (gestrichelt), jedoch nicht unbedingt im **Kritischen Bericht** aufgeführt. Wo analoge Stellen innerhalb eines Satzes mehrmals auftreten, ist der Vorschlag der Herausgeber nur beim ersten Mal abgedruckt, siehe z. B. **Sonate I, Fuga**, Takt 1; **Siciliana**, Takt 1; siehe auch die folgenden Abschnitte unter *Allgemeine Bemerkungen*).

## Die Transkription für Viola

Die vorliegende Transkription transponiert alle Stücke eine Quinte nach unten, ohne dass weitere Änderungen vorgenommen wurden. Die angegebenen Tonhöhen entsprechen immer jenen der transponierten Version für die Viola, auch wenn sie sich auf die Quellen beziehen. Obwohl es für die *Sei Soli* eine maßgebliche Hauptquelle gibt, gestaltete sich die Editionsarbeit nicht so einfach, wie dies zunächst erscheinen mag. Hinsichtlich der Vortragsanweisungen gibt es zahlreiche Mehrdeutigkeiten, die einer Interpretation bedürfen. Dies gilt insbesondere für Bindebögen, die häufig nicht eindeutig platziert sind. Überwiegend stellen sie praktische Angaben zur Strichbezeichnung dar, teilweise kommt ihnen eher die analytische Funktion zu, harmonische und kontrapunktische Fortschreitungen zu visualisieren. Ziel dieser Ausgabe ist es, Bratschisten einen praxisbezogenen Notentext zu bieten, der das Original so weit wie möglich wiedergibt, jedoch auch, wo notwendig, gemäß der barocken Aufführungspraxis und der Umsetzbarkeit für die Viola Interpretationshilfen gibt.

Es wäre schade, wenn sich Bratschisten aufgrund technischer Schwierigkeiten, die auf der Violine weniger problematisch sind, von bestimmten Stücken abhalten ließen und sich lediglich auf die leichteren Sätze beschränken würden. Zwei- oder mehrstimmige Passagen können, wenn man sie notengetreu wiedergeben möchte, für die Viola mitunter nahezu unspielbar erscheinen. Hier wird von den Bratschisten etwas Einfallsreichtum gefordert. Als Beispiel eines Lösungsvorschlags einer solchen Passage ist im Anhang das Beispiel 3 abgedruckt.

Auf der Bratsche bereiten insbesondere die drei- und vierstimmigen Akkorde oft Schwierigkeiten, weil sie schwer und aggressiv klingen können. Es empfiehlt sich daher, die Akkorde generell als Arpeggien auszuführen. Im Hinblick auf Akkorde und die Ausdrucksgebung durch die rechte Hand lohnt es sich, über die Verwendung eines Barockbogens nachzudenken. Bei der Verwendung eines modernen Bogens kann das leichtere Gefühl eines Barockbogens jedoch zumindest teilweise simuliert werden, indem der Bogen weiter oben, knapp hinter dem Daumenleder gehalten wird. Man sollte außerdem im Auge behalten, dass polyphone Passagen üblicherweise eine einzige führende Linie aufweisen, welche es herauszuarbeiten gilt. Alles Weitere kann dann entsprechend angepasst werden. Man kann annehmen, dass die Streicher der Barockzeit die Polyphonie durch Brechung der Akkorde und Nuancen mittels Dynamik andeuten konnten.

Heute herrscht unter historisch kundigen Spielern Konsens, Akkorde mit führender Stimme im Bass wie andere Akkorde auch, d. h. von unten nach oben, zu spielen (zum Beispiel **Sonate I, Siciliana**, Takt 4, dritter Taktschlag).[3] Angesichts der Unmöglichkeit, Passagen mit melodieführender Oberstimme (z. B. **Siciliana**, zu Beginn von Takt 5) von oben nach unten zu spielen, ist auch nicht anzunehmen, dass der Akkord auf dem dritten Taktschlag in Takt 4 oder am Anfang von Takt 19 nach unten gebrochen werden sollte.[4]

Schließlich soll hier daran erinnert werden, dass große Spannen, die auf der Viola naturgemäß noch größer ausfallen, ohne Vibrato oft leichter zu bewerkstelligen sind, obwohl das Vibrato zweifellos ein wichtiger Bestandteil eines angemessen nuancierten Ausdrucks ist.[5]

## Legatobögen und Bogenführung

### Das Adagio der Sonate I

Ein Großteil der Probleme bei der Interpretation des Bach'schen Notentexts resultiert aus Fragen zu den Legatobögen und der entsprechenden Bogenführung. Am stärksten ausgeprägt ist das Problem im Adagio der Sonate I (siehe Faksimileabbildung). Es beginnt bereits in Takt 1: Der Bindebogen auf dem zweiten Viertel ist offenkundig zu kurz; er sollte wohl die ganze Gruppe dieser Zählzeit umfassen. Trotz der besonderen Sorgfalt, mit der Bach Vortragsanweisungen in den Soli notierte, sind die Stellen, an denen Bindebögen beginnen und enden sollten, nicht selten unklar. Zur Interpretation vieler Bindebögen sind Erfahrungen bezüglich der Notationsgewohnheiten Bachs und der Konvention der barocken Bogenführung erforderlich. Als Richtlinie für den Adagio-Satz, in dem manche Legatobögen mehrdeutig oder gar unlogisch erscheinen, kann ein Bogenstrich pro Viertel gelten.

Sodann fehlt ein Bindebogen in Takt 1, dritte Zählzeit, beim Vorhalt von der Septime zur Sexte. Bach notierte keineswegs jeden einzelnen Legatobogen, sondern überließ vieles dem Spieler. Der Vorhalt ist Teil des Themas und ist sonst überall mit einem Legatobogen versehen. Das Legato von einem Vorhalt zu dessen Auflösung war

---

[3] Im $\frac{12}{8}$-Takt ist ein Taktschlag auf ♪. bezogen.

[4] Weiteres zur Ausführung von Akkordbrechungen zu Bachs Zeiten findet sich bei D. Boyden, *The History of Violin Playing from its Origins to 1761*, S. 435–38.

[5] Eine eingehende Erörterung zum Gebrauch des Vibratos in der Barockzeit findet sich bei G. Moens-Haenen, *Das Vibrato in der Musik des Barock*.

eine Aufführungskonvention, ebenso wie die Legatoausführung eines Trillers bis zur Schlussnote (siehe auch erste Zählzeit Takt 10). Im Allgemeinen notierte Bach nur das Wesentliche und überließ allgemeinere Angelegenheiten den Interpreten.

Der Bogen in der ersten Hälfte des zweiten Taktes ist als Legatoangabe insofern ein Problem, als er, wenn man auf der angebundenen Note beginnt, nicht nur einen extrem langen Bogenstrich erfordert, sondern auch einen unerwünschten Aufstrich auf dem Akkord auf der dritten Zählzeit nach sich zieht. Er ist daher am besten als analytischer Bogen zu interpretieren und signalisiert, dass die erste Hälfte des Taktes eine verzierte Auflösung der Septime auf dem ersten Schlag ($f'$) zum $eb'$ auf dem dritten Schlag darstellt. Welcher Bogenstrich auch gewählt wird – er sollte diesen Effekt zum Ausdruck bringen. Die ausgedehnte Verzierung in der zweiten Hälfte des dritten Takts umspielt die Septime ($g'$), welche sich mit dem Triller am Taktende in ein $f'$ auflöst. In diesem Fall muss der Bogen auf der angebundenen Note ansetzen. Bach hat ihn leicht nach rechts gesetzt, vermutlich um ein unsauberes Zusammentreffen mit dem ♭-Vorzeichen zu vermeiden.

Ein ähnlicher Fall, bei dem Bachs Notationsgewohnheiten zu berücksichtigen sind, ist der dritte Schlag in Takt 4. Bach strebte an, alles möglichst nahe am Notensystem zu notieren und keine Bögen zu setzen, die mit Akzidenzien, Notenhälsen oder Fähnchen kollidieren. Nach einem Akkord begann er den Bogen häufig etwas zu weit rechts. Solche Stellen werden von Herausgebern unterschiedlich interpretiert, entweder wirklich als 1+3 Noten oder umgedeutet als 3+1. Eine weitere gute Vorgehensweise besteht darin, sich die Passage ohne den Akkord vorzustellen und sich zu fragen, welche Bogenführung die führende Linie im Takt am besten als Ganzes zur Geltung bringen würde. (Siehe hierzu auch Takt 5, dritter Schlag und Takt 17, dritter Schlag; außerdem **Fuga**, Takt 12, erster Schlag, Takt 57, vierter Schlag; weitere Beispiele finden sich in **Sonate II, Grave**, Takt 7, dritter Schlag; **Partita I, Sarabande**, Takt 5, dritter Schlag; **Partita II, Sarabande**, Takt 7, dritter Schlag; **Ciaccona**, Takte 4, 5, 252, 253).

Das Zurückholen des Bogens kann einen dramatischen Effekt bewirken. Ab Beginn von Takt 20 steigt die Linie von der tiefsten Saite zu einem eindrucksvollen Quartvorhaltsklang auf (dritter Schlag Takt 21), was zu einer kulminierenden Kadenzwirkung führt. Aufeinanderfolgende Abstriche können zahlreiche Artikulationen ermöglichen – vom dramatischen Akzent bis etwa zu einer Stelle wie Takt 6 der **Gavotte en rondeaux Partita III**), wo die leichte Unterbrechung, die durch das Zurückholen des Bogens entsteht, quasi erwünscht ist, während die halbe Note in Takt 2 eher ein Vorangehen fordert.

*Allgemeine Bemerkungen*

Es ist mitunter angebracht, Noten zu binden, auch wenn sie in den Quellen nicht mit einem Bindebogen versehen sind, etwa, wenn in zwei Stimmen Achtel und Viertel kombiniert werden. Im Allgemeinen eignen sich Legatobögen für kleine Intervalle wie Sekunden und Terzen, für größere Intervalle sah Bach sie jedoch vermutlich nicht vor (siehe z. B. **Partita I, Sarabande**, Takt 3, wo auf dem zweiten und dritten Viertel durchaus gebunden werden könnte, auf dem ersten jedoch eher nicht).

Bögen, die im Zusammenhang mit der Triolenziffer *3* stehen (siehe z. B. die **Allemanda** in den **Partiten I und II**), sind nicht unbedingt als Legatobögen zu verstehen. Wie Leopold Mozart in Kapitel VI seiner *Violinschule* nahelegt, kann ein und dieselbe Grundfigur unterschiedlich gestrichen werden.[6] Das Gleiche gilt für Triolen und Dreiergruppen ohne jegliche Bögen, wie etwa in **Partita I, Double der Sarabande**. In diesem Satz sind im Autograph Bögen ober- und unterhalb des letzten Taktes vor der Wiederholung ("chapeaux") notiert, diese haben die Funktion der Wiederholungsklammer 1.

Bögen zur Kennzeichnung eines gebundenen Trillers (siehe *Verzierungen*) sind sehr verbreitet; sie können aber zu ungünstiger Bogenführung verleiten. Die Vorschläge des Herausgebers wollen hierzu Lösungen anbieten (siehe **Partita I, Allemanda**, Takt 7, vierter Schlag usw., **Sonate II, Grave**, Takt 2, zweiter Schlag usw.).

In der **Sonate I, Siciliana** läßt sich die vom Herausgeber vorgeschlagene Kombination von Ab-Auf-Ab-Auf-Auf-Strich am Beginn bequem ausführen, in der Sequenz in den Takten 9ff. kann jedoch eine Kombination von Ab-Auf-Auf-Ab-Auf-Strich vorzuziehen sein, da sie einen profilierteren Vortrag ermöglicht.

Fugenthemen bedürfen einer sorgfältigen Betrachtung. In **Sonate I, Fuga** sind die zwei Sechzehntel im Thema mit zwei Aufstrichen ausführbar, dies mag jedoch innerhalb des vorherrschenden Canzona-Charakters als zu leicht empfunden werden. Daher wurde vom Herausgeber die Abfolge Ab-Ab-Auf vorgeschlagen. Mit zunehmender Mehrstimmigkeit (Takt 3 usw.) kann eine Kombination von Ab-Auf-Auf-Strichen den Akkorden mehr Ausdruck verleihen. In der **Fuga** von **Sonate II** ist die am Anfang des Satzes natürliche Abfolge von Ab-Auf-Ab-Strich problemlos auf den Rest des Satzes übertragbar. Die für die **Fuga** in **Sonate III** vorgeschlagenen Striche für das Thema, die bei den aufeinanderfolgenden Abstrichen möglichst ohne großes Zurückholen des Bogens auszuführen sind, sorgen für einen ruhigeren und stärker geordneten Effekt als bei Ganzbogenstrichen. Dies dient als Wegbereitung zu der anschließenden sehr umfangreichen Fuge. Mit zunehmender Mehrstimmigkeit wird diese Bogenführung nicht mehr uneingeschränkt möglich sein, und jeder, der diese spielerische Meisterleistung vollbringen will, muss mit Einfallsreichtum andere Lösungen finden. In den wiegenden Orgelpunktpassagen ab Takt 186 erzeugen die Strichwechsel eine größere Resonanz, wenn sie alle Achtel anstatt Viertel vollzogen werden.

In den zahlreichen Fällen in der **Allemanda, Partita 1**, wo auf eine punktierte Note zwei Zweiunddreißigstel folgen, sind je nach gewünschtem Effekt unterschiedliche Bogenführungen möglich. Georg Muffat schlägt vor, entweder alle Noten einzeln zu streichen oder alternativ für einen „sanfteren" Klang die beiden schnellen Noten zusammen mit der punktierten Note auf einem Bogen zu nehmen oder aber die beiden kurzen Noten als Paar zu streichen – je nachdem, „wie es angemessen scheint".[7]

---

[6] Leopold Mozarts *Versuch einer gründlichen Violinschule* ist in Bezug auf Bachs Musik keineswegs als eine zu spät erschienene Veröffentlichung anzusehen. Sie wurde vier Jahre nach Quantzs *Versuch* veröffentlicht und basierte auf früheren Veröffentlichungen von Tartini. Im Mittelpunkt steht der italienische Stil, wohingegen Quantz auch viel über das Musizieren im französischen Stil zu sagen hatte.

[7] G. Muffat, *Florilegium secundum*, siehe D. K. Wilson, *Georg Muffat on Performance Practice*, S. 40; W. Kolneder, *Georg Muffat zur Aufführungspraxis*, S. 64–67.

Einige Bögen sind eher als analytische Phrasierungsbögen anstatt als Artikulationsbögen zu betrachten, so etwa im oben genannten Beispiel des **Adagios** aus **Sonate I**, Takt 2. Ein anderes Beispiel findet sich im **Largo** der **Sonate III**, Takt 19, wo der lange Bogen ein Verklingen impliziert und nicht unbedingt als Artikulationsbogen zu verstehen ist.

### *Kontrapunkt*

Bachs kontrapunktische Notation für ein solistisches Saiteninstrument stellt eher eine ideale kontrapunktische Textur dar als etwas, das genau wie notiert zu spielen ist. Diese Tatsache haben die Verfechter des alten Vega-/Bach-Bogens, der es der Violine ermöglichen sollte, wie eine Orgel zu klingen, nicht gesehen. Die Kunst besteht darin, den Inhaltsreichtum des Kontrapunkts überzeugend zum Ausdruck zu bringen. Beispielsweise gibt es oft mehrstimmige Stellen mit einer Stimme in kürzeren und einer anderen in längeren Noten. In solchen Fällen wird man die schnelleren Noten gebunden spielen, wie in der **Fuga** von **Sonate I**, Takt 15–18 (**Anhang** Beispiel 1) und in **Sonate III**, **Fuga**, Takt 115–121 (**Anhang** Beispiel 6). Legatobögen können auch alternative Bogenstriche kennzeichnen, wie in weiten Teilen im **Andante** der **Sonate II** (**Anhang** Beispiel 4). Das Verkürzen gebundener Töne kann (auf der Bratsche) einen unbequemen Griff in der linken Hand erleichtern, wie in **Sonate II**, **Fuga**, Takt 128–130 (**Anhang** Beispiel 3). In der **Fuga** von **Sonate III** werden in Takt 161–162 die beiden Unterstimmen wohl mit einem Bogenwechsel gestrichen werden müssen, und es besteht keine Möglichkeit, die Oberstimme zu halten.

In **Sonate III**, **Adagio** sollte die Bogenführung mit einem Strich pro Viertel, wo immer dies praktisch möglich ist, den ganzen Satz hindurch beibehalten werden. In den Takten 34–36 können die langen Noten in der oberen Stimme wieder verkürzt gehalten werden. Dieses Stück ist ein gutes Beispiel für die Notwendigkeit, die Bogenführung entsprechend der individuellen Möglichkeiten des Interpreten zu gestalten.

Die Töne des chromatischen Kontrasubjekts in den Takten 4ff. der **Fuga** (**Sonate III**) müssen leicht voneinander abgesetzt, nicht gebunden und alle mit der gleichen Länge gespielt werden. Dasselbe gilt für **Sonate II**, **Fuga**, Takte 5ff.

## Verzierungen

Es gibt mehrere Einführungen in die Ornamentik der Barockzeit.[8] In seinem *Clavier-Büchlein* für Wilhelm Friedemann Bach (siehe **Anhang** Beispiel 8) gab Bach eine kurze Erklärung seiner Verzierungssymbole. Es handelt sich um eine Tabelle mit dreizehn Verzierungen aus dem Jahr 1720 – jenem Jahr, mit dem auch das Autograph der *Soli* datiert ist. Dennoch hat Bach den Sonaten und Partiten offensichtlich einen eigenen Referenzstatus zuerkannt; er benutzte nur ein Verzierungszeichen (*tr* für einen Triller), während er andere wesentliche Verzierungen der Ausführung der Spieler überließ.[9] Da er jedoch grundsätzlich sorgfältig notierte, schrieb er die komplexeren Verzierungen in Noten aus. Bei der Interpretation der reichverzierten langsamen Sätze lohnt es sich, Bachs Verzierungstabelle von 1720 heranzuziehen, da die Imaginierung eines Verzierungszeichens zu den Noten mit dabei helfen kann, zierende Notengruppen mit der notwendigen Freiheit zu gestalten.

Triller beginnen im Allgemeinen mit einer betonten oberen Nebennote, doch es gibt viele Fälle, wo der verzierten Note im Legato eine Note eine Sekunde höher vorausgeht, sodass sich ein angebundener Triller ergibt. Bei absteigenden Tonschritten werden Triller üblicherweise im Legato als Verzierung, d. h. in kürzerem Notenwert und ohne obere Nebennote gespielt, da dies die Linie unterbrechen würde. Ein typisches Beispiel ist Takt 6, dritte Zählzeit, im **Largo** (**Sonate III**), später, in Takt 16 hat Bach den implizierten Bindebogen notiert. Ein anderer Fall ist in der **Partita I**, **Allemanda**, Takt 2, zweiter Schlag gegeben, wo das *g'* an das *f♯'* gebunden werden könnte und der Triller aus nur drei Noten besteht (zum Charakter dieses Stückes siehe Abschnitt *Gemischter Stil*, weiter unten).

Zwei Verzierungsfiguren, die in den Soli häufig vorkommen, finden sich in der **Sonata II**, **Grave**, Takt 2 auf der zweiten und dritten Zählzeit. Die erste ist im Grunde ein zusammengesetztes Ornament aus einem Vorschlag, einem Triller und einem Mordent. Bei schnellen Notenwerten, wie den hier gegebenen Zweiunddreißigsteln, besteht der Triller mitunter aus nur drei Noten – die obere Nebennote *e'* ist gedanklich an die Achtel-Appoggiatura gebunden (siehe Notenbeispiel). Es handelt sich hier um eine feine Verzierung, bei der der Vorschlag akzentuiert wird und die restlichen Töne dieser Zählzeit zurückgenommen werden.

Die zweite Figur, jene auf der dritten Zählzeit, hat einen einfachen Triller, doch dieses Mal geht dem Triller auf dem *c'* die Obersekunde *d'* voraus. Dies erfolgt genau auf den Taktschlag von einer kürzeren auf eine längere Note, sodass das *d'* wiederholt werden sollte (die Figur in diesem Schlag ist eine Version des *coulé de tierce*, siehe *Andere Notationsformen*).

Vorhaltsnoten sollten betont und legato mit ihrer (leichter zu nehmenden) Hauptnote verbunden werden. In **Partita 3**, **Loure**, Takt 6 ff. nehmen die Vorhalte das Gewicht von der Hauptnote. Triller, die auf Auflösungstönen erfolgen, sollten daher sehr leicht genommen werden, wie etwa in **Sonate I**, **Adagio**, Takt 4, erste Zählzeit.

Für den Triller innerhalb einer Kadenz gibt François Couperin einen Lösungsansatz, der generell hilfreich ist. Der Triller besteht aus drei Komponenten: (a) der Appoggiatura (*appuy*), die betont werden sollte; (b) den Tonwiederholungen, die gemächlich begonnen und dann schneller werden sollten und (c) dem Haltepunkt (*point d'arrêt*), welcher mit der zweiten Achtel im Bass zusammenfallen sollte (die Tonwiederholungen enden also auf der Punktierung). Die Antizipation des letzten Tonika-Tons (*d*) sollte kurz gespielt werden.[10]

---

[8] Das Thema ist nicht unumstritten. Gute, prägnante Einführungen in Bachs Verzierungen geben W. Emery in *Bach's Ornaments* und H. Klotz in *Die Ornamentik der Klavier- und Orgelwerke von Johann Sebastian Bach*. In beiden findet sich ein Nachdruck von Bachs Tabelle aus dem Jahr 1720, und Klotz liefert viele weitere Tabellen aus Bachs Umfeld.

[9] Auffällig ist das Fehlen wesentlicher Verzierungszeichen im Vergleich mit Bachs autographer Einrichtung der Partita III für die „Laute" (BWV 1006a), auffällig, siehe *Gemischter Stil* (weiter unten).

[10] F. Couperin, *L'Art de toucher le clavecin*, S. 24.

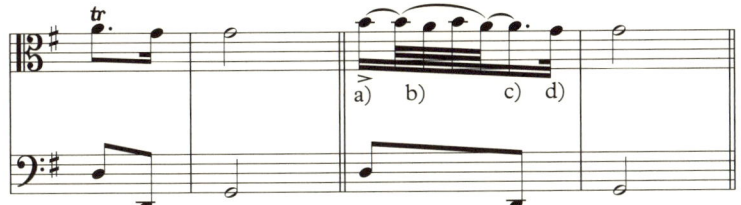

Eine Haltebogen-Version davon hat Bach in der **Sonate III, Adagio**, Takt 14 notiert. An dieser Stelle ein Trillerzeichen über das *d'* zu setzen, gehörte zu den konventionellen Dingen, die Bach nicht immer zu notieren bemüht war. Die Vorhaltsnote *eb'* wird an dieser Stelle an die erste Note des Trillers gebunden.

## Andere Notationsformen

Bis Mitte der 1720er Jahre notierte Bach im Dreiertakt häufig kleine Taktstriche. In **Sonate I, Presto** verleihen sie dem Satz einen energischeren Charakter als ein ⁶⁄₈-Takt dies tun würde und betonen zudem die Polyrhythmie. In der **Corrente** von **Partita I** vermitteln sie den Eindruck von starken und schwachen Takten, was durch wechselnde Strichmuster zum Ausdruck kommt.

Punktierungen haben in dieser Musik nicht nur die Funktion, eine Note zu verlängern, sondern können auch einen Akzent implizieren.[11] Dies wird deutlich in **Partita II, Corrente**, wo als einziges Mal punktierte Viertelnoten im Akkord in Takt 49 vorkommen. Hier, auf dem erreichten Höhepunkt, impliziert die Punktierung einen Akzent und eine kurze Fermate. Solche quasi akzentuierten punktierten Noten sind häufig in der musikalischen Figur der Tirata zu finden. In **Sonate II, Grave**, Takt 1, vierter Schlag wird die Tirata als Teil des motivischen Gewebes des Satzes vorgestellt. In Takt 5 wird sie zur dreifachen Tirata ausgeweitet, die zum Höhepunkt in Takt 6 führt. Die punktierte Noten symbolisieren einen Akzent mit kurzer Pause, nicht einen genauen Wert. Auf eine Tirata aus vier Noten folgt eine aus sechs Noten und eine eher konventionelle Schlussverzierung. Viele Herausgeber tendieren dazu, an dieser Stelle Bachs Notation zu ändern, und streichen in Takt 5, vierte Zählzeit, häufig die Punktierung beim *a'*. Bachs Notation in der zweiten Hälfte von Takt 5 mag nicht aufgehen, sie vermittelt jedoch eine entscheidende expressive Nuance.

Die Wellenlinien am Ende der **Sonate II, Grave** sind auf unterschiedliche Weise interpretiert worden.[12] Die naheliegendste Deutung scheint ein dezentes Ondeggiando zu sein – ein schneller, schwankender Effekt beim Doppelgriff, der durch eine an- und abschwellende Strichstärke erzeugt wird, ohne die beiden Töne dabei zu unterbrechen. Die Wellenlinien enden auf der zweiten Viertel, wo das Ondeggiando in der Oberstimme zu einem Triller wird. Das Ziel sollte es sein, den dramatischen Effekt der phrygischen Kadenz, die die **Fuga** vorbereitet, zu steigern. Die Fuge sollte sofort beginnen (es ist keine Fermate notiert), denn das Thema greift die Oktavdominante auf und führt sie im zweiten Takt zur Tonika.

Das **Adagio** der **Sonate I** endet mit einer authentischen Kadenz und einer Fermate auf dem Schlussakkord, daher kann dort vor der Fuge eine kleine Pause sein. Demgegenüber enden die **ersten Sätze** der **Sonaten II und III** mit einem Halbschluss. Bach notierte hier keine Fermate und schrieb die Taktangabe für die Fuge unmittelbar hinter den Doppelstrich der letzten Zeile, ein Hinweis, dass die Fuge sofort anzuschließen ist.

## Gemischter Stil

Die deutschen Lande waren im späteren 17. Jahrhundert ein Schmelztiegel musikalischer Stile. Die vielen Höfe, die bemüht waren, mit der Mode Schritt zu halten, verpflichteten französische, italienische sowie deutsche Musiker. Der in musikalischer Hinsicht fortschrittlichste Hof in Bachs Umgebung befand sich in Dresden. Zu den vielen dort beschäftigten Musikern zählte J. B. Volumier, der ein französisches Orchester leitete, der führende italienische Geigenvirtuose F. M. Veracini sowie der fortschrittliche und kundige deutsche Violinist J. G. Pisendel, der in Bezug auf die unterschiedlichen Stile äußerst bewandert war. Mit den Soli verfolgte Bach auch das Ziel, den deutschen gemischten Stil zu vertreten, welcher vor allem Stilmomente aus französischer und italienischer Musik mit einbezog, aber auch polnische und englische Einflüsse hatte.[13]

Jedes einzelne der sechs Soli präsentiert eine Version des gemischten Stils, und diese Vielfalt verleiht den Stücken den Rang eines Kompendiums für die Kenner musikalischer Stile und Techniken. In der **Fuga** der **Sonate II** beispielsweise verbindet Bach ein leichtes französisches Tanzmetrum (*bourrée*) mit Fugentechnik und kleidet es in das Gewand eines italienischen Concertos mit konzertanten Figurationen, Bariolage und sogar Echos – eine für Bach sehr charakteristische Mischung.

Alle drei Partiten zeigen in meisterlicher Weise die verschiedenen Stilmomente auf. In der **Allemanda** der **Partita I** stehen dem metrischen Stil einer kunstvollen französischen Allemande die laufenden Sechzehntel ihres Doubles gegenüber, welche der italienischen Sonatentradition entstammen – es ist, als ob sich François Couperin und Arcangelo Corelli begegneten.[14] Es ist wichtig, dies zu verstehen, denn die weiten Sprünge und der punktierte Rhythmus der Allemanda können auch aggressiv und dissonant aufgefasst werden. Von der französischen Tradition aus betrachtet handelt es sich eindeutig um einen Satz im *Style brisé* (arpeggierter Kontrapunkt mit zwei Stimmen in einer) mit ausgeschriebenen *Notes inégales*. Eine typische französische Allemande steht im 𝄴-Takt, und die Ausführung der Sechzehntel erfolgt ungleichmäßig. Solche *Notes inégales*, von scharf punktiert bis zu sanft triolisch, sind am besten als ein Ausdrucksmittel zu verstehen. Der Grad der ungleichmäßigen Ausführung ist eine Frage des persönlichen Empfindens und abhängig von der speziellen Stilmischung eines Stücks und ihrem Ausdrucksmoment. Offenkundig wird diese stilistische Besonderheit vor dem Hintergrund der französischen Lautentradition,

---

[11] Siehe J. J. Quantz, *Versuch einer Anweisung die Flöte traversiere zu spielen*, XVII vii §56 und 58.

[12] Eine Übersicht möglicher Interpretationen findet sich bei D. Ledbetter, *Unaccompanied Bach : Performing the Solo Works*, S. 121f.; siehe auch G. Moens-Haenen, *Zur Frage der Wellenlinien in der Musik Johann Sebastian Bachs*.

[13] Bachs Bemerkung zu den Dresdner Musikern sind in *NBR*, S. 150 nachzulesen; eine detailliertere Erläuterung der Hauptelemente des gemischten Stils findet sich bei D. Ledbetter, *Unaccompanied Bach : Performing the Solo Works*, Chapter Two.

[14] Zur weiteren Erörterung des stilistischen Hintergrunds siehe die Ausführungen zu diesem Stück in D. Ledbetter, *Unaccompanied Bach : Performing the Solo Works*.

mit der die unbegleitete barocke Streichermusik viel gemeinsam hat.¹⁵ Bachs Hinzufügung sind Triolen im galanten Stil. Zierende Notengruppen in komplexer Vielfalt waren ein Merkmal dieses Stils, der sich um 1720 ausprägte.

**Partita I** ist für sich genommen ein Kompendium der Notenwerte und Tempoverhältnisse. Die Taktangabe ¢ in der Allemanda Double impliziert das doppelte Tempo der Allemanda c (♩ = ♪). Die Corrente, die mit ihrem durchgängig verkleinerten Notenwert (Achtel) bereits im Stil der italienischen Sonate steht, hat dieselbe Taktangabe 3/4 und dasselbe Tempo wie ihr Double. Die Sarabande und ihr triolisch geführtes Double haben ungefähr dasselbe Tempo, obwohl das Double hier zu einem fließenderen Tempo einlädt. Ungewöhnlich an der Sarabande ist das Fehlen einer Betonung der zweiten Zählzeit. Mehrfach findet sich ein Bindebogen über drei Achteln (Takt 10 usw.), ein rhythmisches Äquivalent zur punktierten Viertel (Takt 2 usw.). Das vorherrschende Metrum von drei gleichwertigen Vierteln und deren auftaktige Wirkung auf eine folgende punktierte Viertel verleiht diesem Satz den Charakter eines Trauermarsches. Die gängige französische *Inegalité* bei den Achteln wäre hier ziemlich unangemessen, doch ein erkennbares Betonungsschema von stark–schwach/betont–unbetont unterstützt die Ausdrucksgebung. Die Tempo di Borea und ihr Double sind sich im Charakter ähnlich. Der verkleinerte Notenwert (Achtel) bekommt im zweiten Teil allmählich mehr Gewicht, bis er im Double endgültig die Oberhand gewinnt.

Auch in der **Partita III** stehen sich unterschiedliche Stile gegenüber. Das **Preludio** ist durch und durch italienisch, die **Loure** durch und durch französisch geprägt. Entsprechend unterscheidet sich die Bogenführung. Die Italiener tendierten zu langen, großen Strichen, die Franzosen neigten dazu, den Bogen häufiger abzuheben und jeden Takt mit Abstrich zu beginnen.¹⁶ Ein französischer Autor der Zeit beschrieb den Unterschied sehr treffend: Die Franzosen spielen mit „in die Luft gehobenem Bogen", während die Italiener „glatte und wohl verbundene Auf- und Abstriche verwenden, deren Wechsel unhörbar sind und endlose Notenketten in einem gleichbleibenden Fluss hervorbringen."¹⁷ Die folgenden Tänze nehmen immer mehr italienische Färbung an. Die **Gavotte** zeigt eine gängige Mischung von Stilen. Tanzrhythmen wechseln sich ab mit längeren Passagen aus laufenden Achtelnoten. Die Zwischenspiele (Couplets) haben Stilmerkmale der Musette, der Sonate und des konzertanten Stils. Das **Menuet I** beginnt im Tanzmetrum, nimmt mit den fortlaufenden Achteln im zweiten Teil jedoch sonatenhafte Züge an. Im **Menuet II** wechseln sich der schlichte Stil einer Musette und der elegante Stil einer Sonate ab. In der **Bourée** laufen die durchgehenden Achtel weiter, eingestreut sind konzertante Echos wie im Preludio, und mit der **Gigue** findet die Rückkehr zum italienischen Stil ihren Abschluss.

Ein wichtiger Aspekt der *Notes inégales* ist die Ausführung der punktierten Rhythmen, etwa in der **Sonate I**, **Siciliana**, Takt 1, erster Schlag und noch mehr in der **Partita III**, **Loure**, Takt 1, erster Schlag. Spielt man diesen Rhythmus wie notiert, fehlt ihm die Spannung, eine leicht abweichende Ausführung ist entscheidend für den Tanzcharakter. Generell empfiehlt es sich, anstelle eines geraden Zweiertaktes in zusammengesetzten Taktarten zu denken, die erste Hälfte von Takt 1 der Loure beispielsweise wie einen 9/8-Takt, in dem die Achtel mit der letzten Note einer Triole zusammenfällt. Das Ziel ist ein anmutig beschwingter Rhythmus, der frei von Schwere ist und nicht ins Stocken gerät. Ein besonderes Problem tritt in der **Ciaccona** der **Partita II** zutage. In einigen älteren Aufführungen wurde der Anfangsakkord auf der folgenden Achtelnote im ersten Takt wiederholt – mit sehr schwerer und schleppender Wirkung. In diesem eröffnenden Teil des Stückes gilt es, etwas von dem beschwingten Rhythmus einer französischen Chaconne zu vermitteln, obwohl das Tempo bedeutend langsamer sein muss, als es bei einer getanzten Chaconne von Lully wäre. Die Kunst ist es, das tänzerische Ausdrucksmoment mit dem ernsten, um nicht zu sagen tragischen Charakter des Satzes zu verbinden, und zwar in einem Tempo, das im späteren Verlauf auch mit demjenigen der virtuosen deutschen und italienischen Stile jener Zeit vereinbar ist. Ein weiterer Fall tritt auf, wenn der notierte Rhythmus nicht aufgeht, wie bei einer punktierten Achtel, auf die drei Zweiunddreißigstel folgen, beispielsweise in der **Partita I**, **Allemanda**, Takt 5, dritte Zählzeit. Hier richtet sich die Ausführung der Zweiunddreißigstel nach der für dieses Stück festgelegten Länge der Punktierung.

Eine sehr charakteristische französische Erscheinung ist der melodische *Coulé de tierce*, der gewöhnlich als Abschluss einer Phrase verwendet wurde. Er entspricht einer kleinen Zäsur oder einer Atempause wie bei Sängern oder Bläsern.¹⁸ Seine unverzierte Form ist die fallende Terz wie in **Partita III**, **Loure**, Takt 1, vierte und fünfte Note. In einem Autograph, das möglicherweise eine Bearbeitung für Laute darstellt, hat Bach zusätzlich die üblichen Verzierungsnoten notiert (siehe **Anhang**, Beispiel 7): Der obere Vorschlag (eine Appoggiatura / *appuy*) würde normalerweise auf dem Schlag erfolgen, der andere (ein *Coulé*) würde vor der tieferen Viertel gespielt und an diese gebunden.¹⁹ Ein *Coulé de tierce* kann in verschiedenen Formen auftreten: In der zweiten Takthälfte von Takt 4 der Loure sind es zwei gepaarte Achtel; in der **Partita I**, **Allemanda**, Takt 5, erste Zählzeit steht er im lombardischen Rhythmus (kurz–lang) – dem Gegenstück der üblichen (lang–kurz gespielten) *Notes inégales*. Er ist ein wichtiges Artikulierungsmittel bei der Gestaltung komplexer Phrasen und kann auch innerhalb von Notenketten in einem stärker italienisch geprägten Stil auftreten, so etwa in der **Partita II**, **Allemanda**, Takt 6, erste Zählzeit, wo er das Ende des ersten musikalischen Gedankens kennzeichnet.

November 2016

*David Ledbetter*
(*Übersetzung: Lore Horlamus*)

---

¹⁵ Zu den Referenzaufnahmen für Laute zählt Nigel Norths frühe Einspielung, die in stilistischer Hinsicht von vielen als eine Offenbarung angesehen wurde (Linn Records CKD 013, 1994).

¹⁶ Siehe G. Muffat, *Florilegium secundum*, Abschnitt II in Wilson, *Georg Muffat on Performance Practice*, insbesondere S. 40; W. Kolneder, *Georg Muffat zur Aufführungspraxis*. S. 66–67.

¹⁷ H. Le Blanc, *Defense de la basse de viole contre les entreprises du violon et les prétentions du violoncel*, siehe D. Ledbetter, *Unaccompanied Bach: Performing the Solo Works*, S. 39.

¹⁸ Nicht zu verwechseln mit *Tierce coulée*, einer Verzierung für Tasteninstrumente, die normalerweise als Zweiklang mit einem Schrägstrich zwischen den Noten notiert ist. Dabei handelt es sich lediglich um eine einem arpeggierten Intervall oder Akkord hinzugefügte Durchgangsnote, die keine melodische Zäsur impliziert.

¹⁹ Hinsichtlich BWV 1006a siehe Anmerkungen in D. Ledbetter, *Unaccompanied Bach: Performing the Solo Works*. BWV 1006a, herausgegeben in NBA V/10. In Takt 1 der Loure (Beispiel 7) hat Bach mit Sicherheit die übliche Ausführung mit *coulé* vor der fünften Note intendiert, um den Einsatz des Basstons *a* auf dem 6. Viertel zu ermöglichen.

# Sonata I
## BWV 1001

J. S. Bach (1685–1750)
Transcribed for Viola
by Simon Rowland-Jones

*) See Preface: Slurs and bowing *The Adagio of Sonata I* / Siehe Vorwort: Legatobögen und Bogenführung, *Sonate I, Adagio*

*) See Preface: Slurs and bowing *General points* / Siehe Vorwort: Legatobögen und Bogenführung, *Allgemeine Bemerkungen*
**) See Preface: Slurs and bowing, *Counterpoint* (See also Appendix: Ex. 1)
    Siehe Vorwort: Legatobögen und Bogenführung, *Kontrapunkt* (siehe auch Anhang, Beispiel 1)

*) See Appendix: Example 2 / Siehe Anhang: Beispiel 2

*) See Preface: Slurs and bowing, *General points* / Siehe Vorwort: Legatobögen und Bogenführung, *Allgemeine Bemerkungen*
**) See Preface: Transcription and the viola / Siehe Vorwort: Die Transkription für Viola

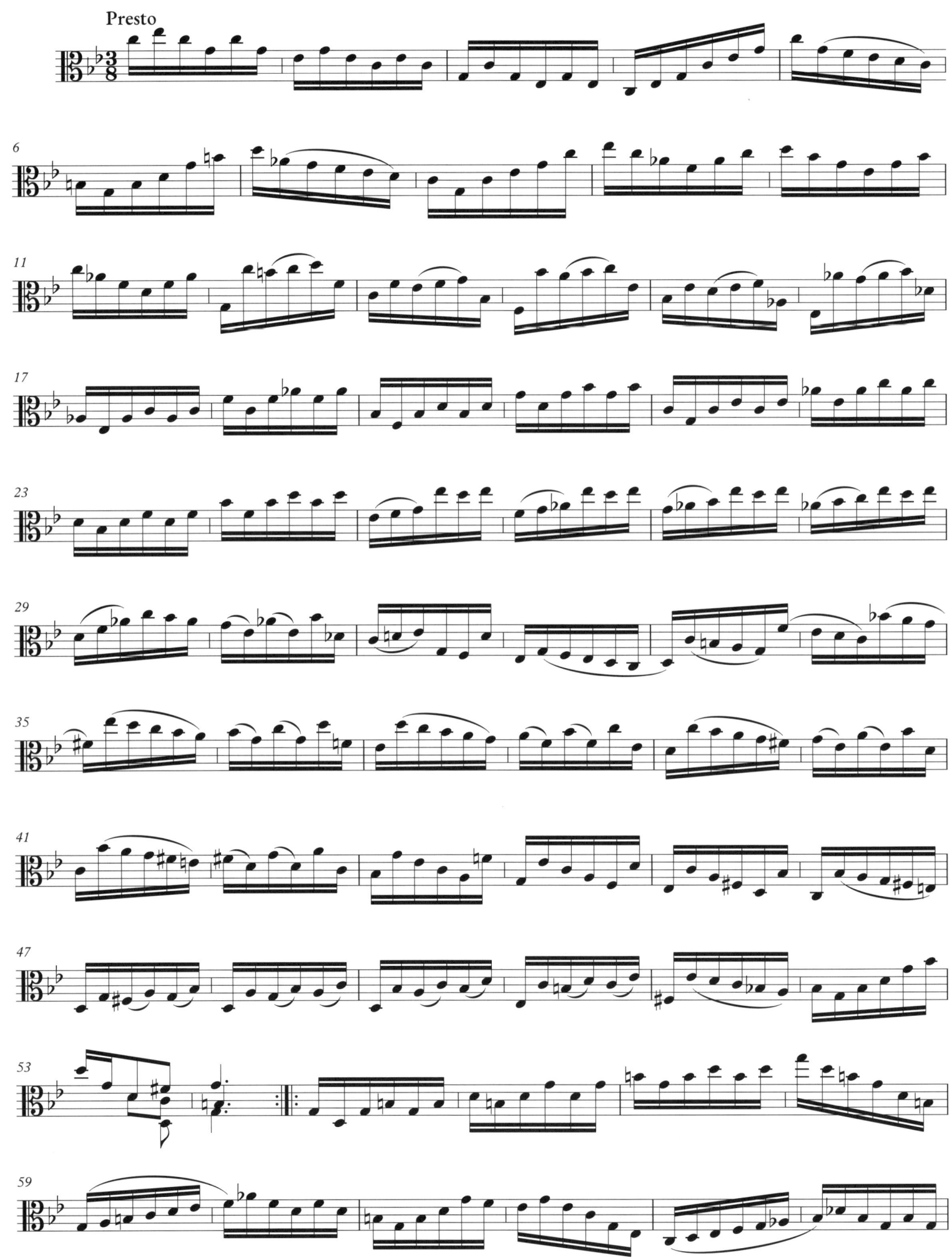

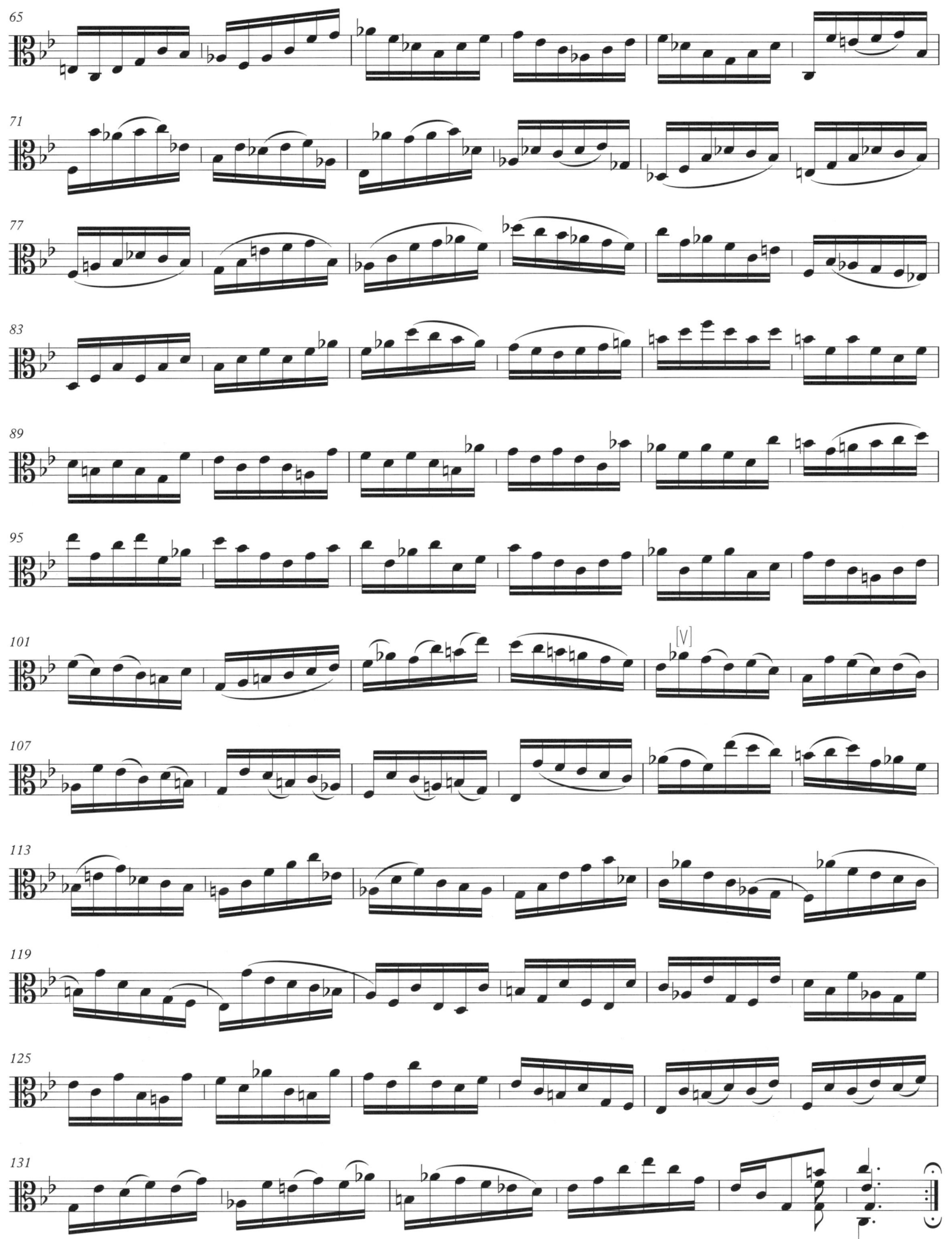

# Partita I
## BWV 1002

Allemanda

*) See Preface: Ornaments / Siehe Vorwort: Verzierungen
**) See Preface: Mixed style / Siehe Vorwort: Gemischter Stil

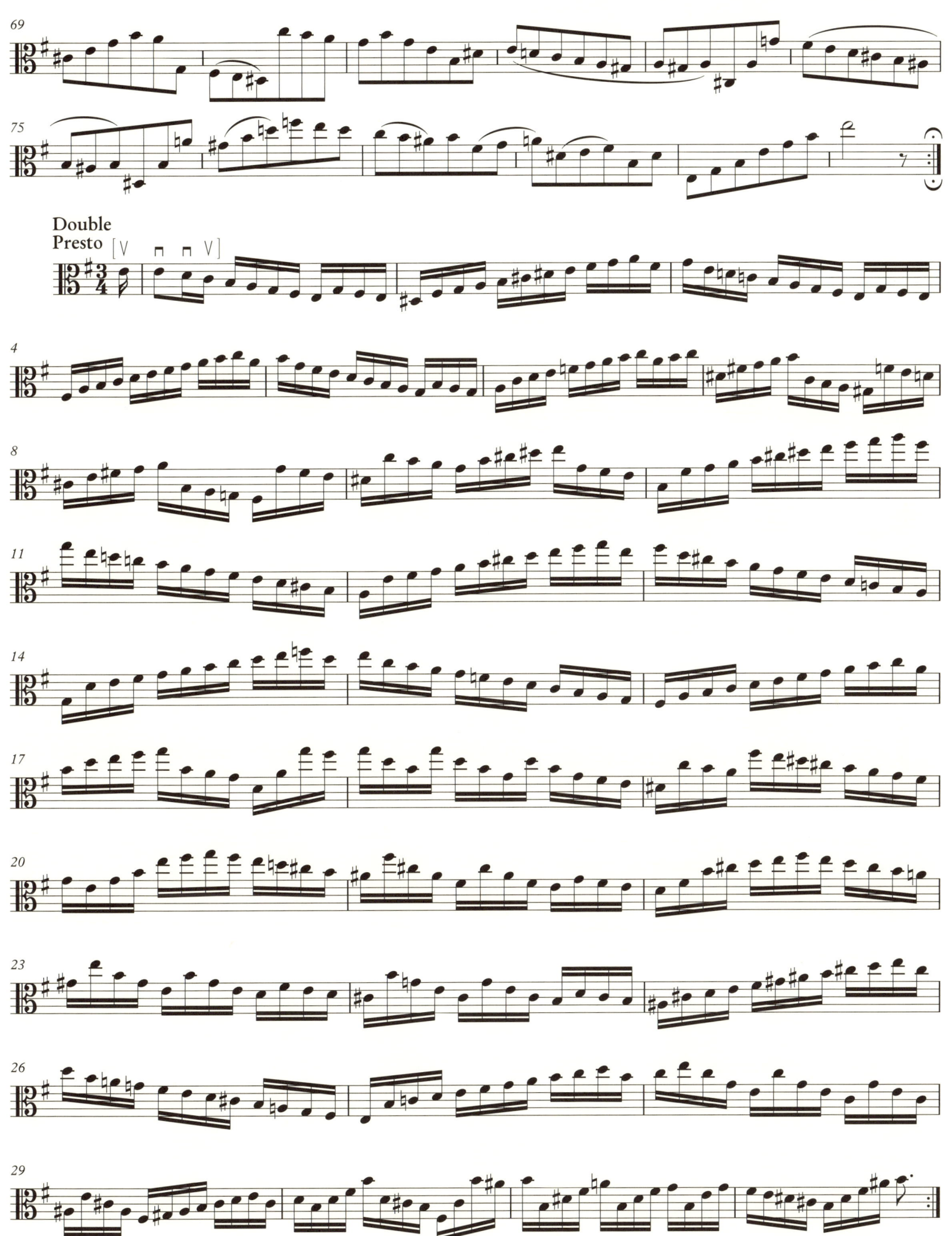

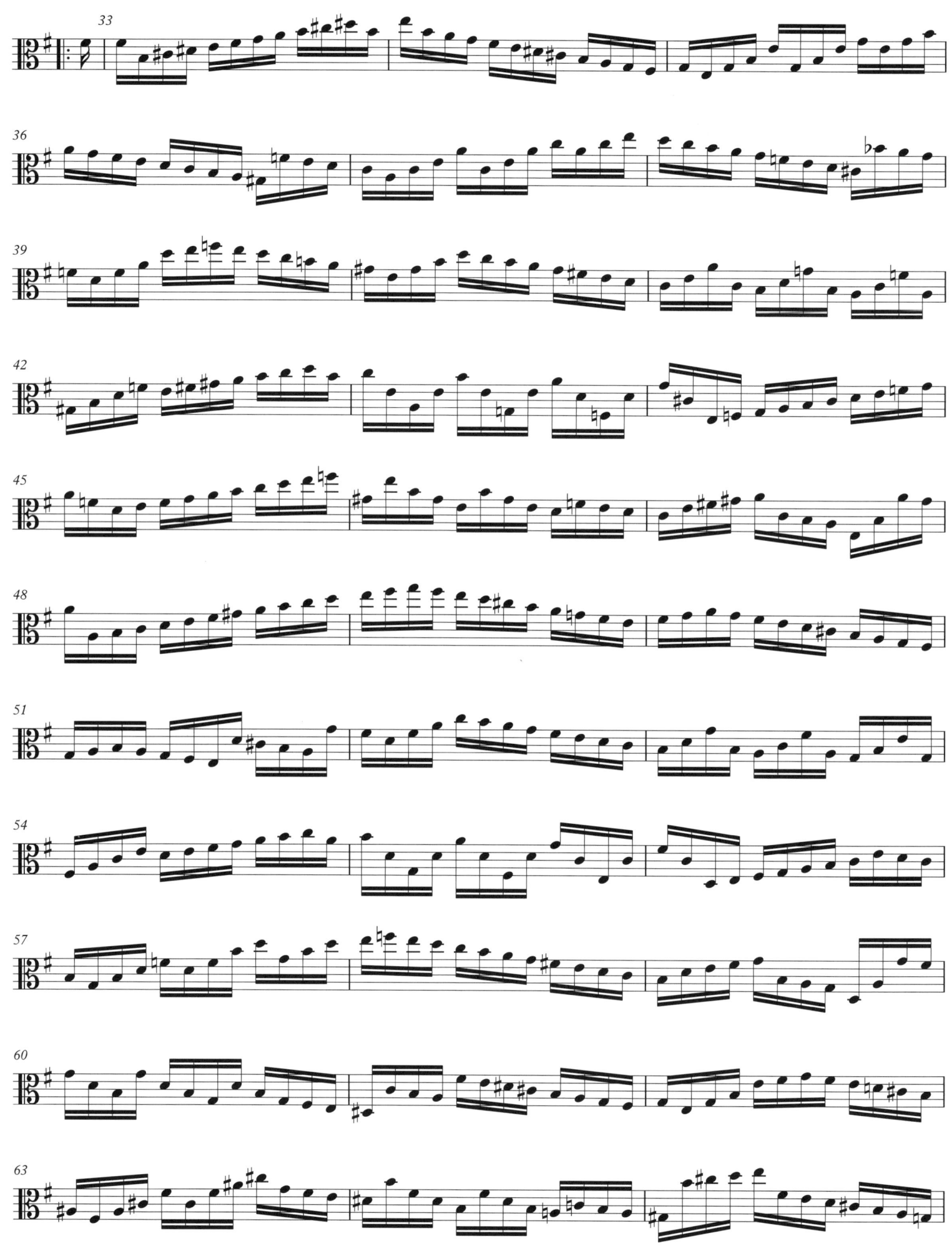

Sarabande

*) See Preface: Slurs and bowing *General Points* / Siehe Vorwort: Legatobögen und Bogenführung *Allgemeine Hinweise*

# Sonata II
## BWV 1003

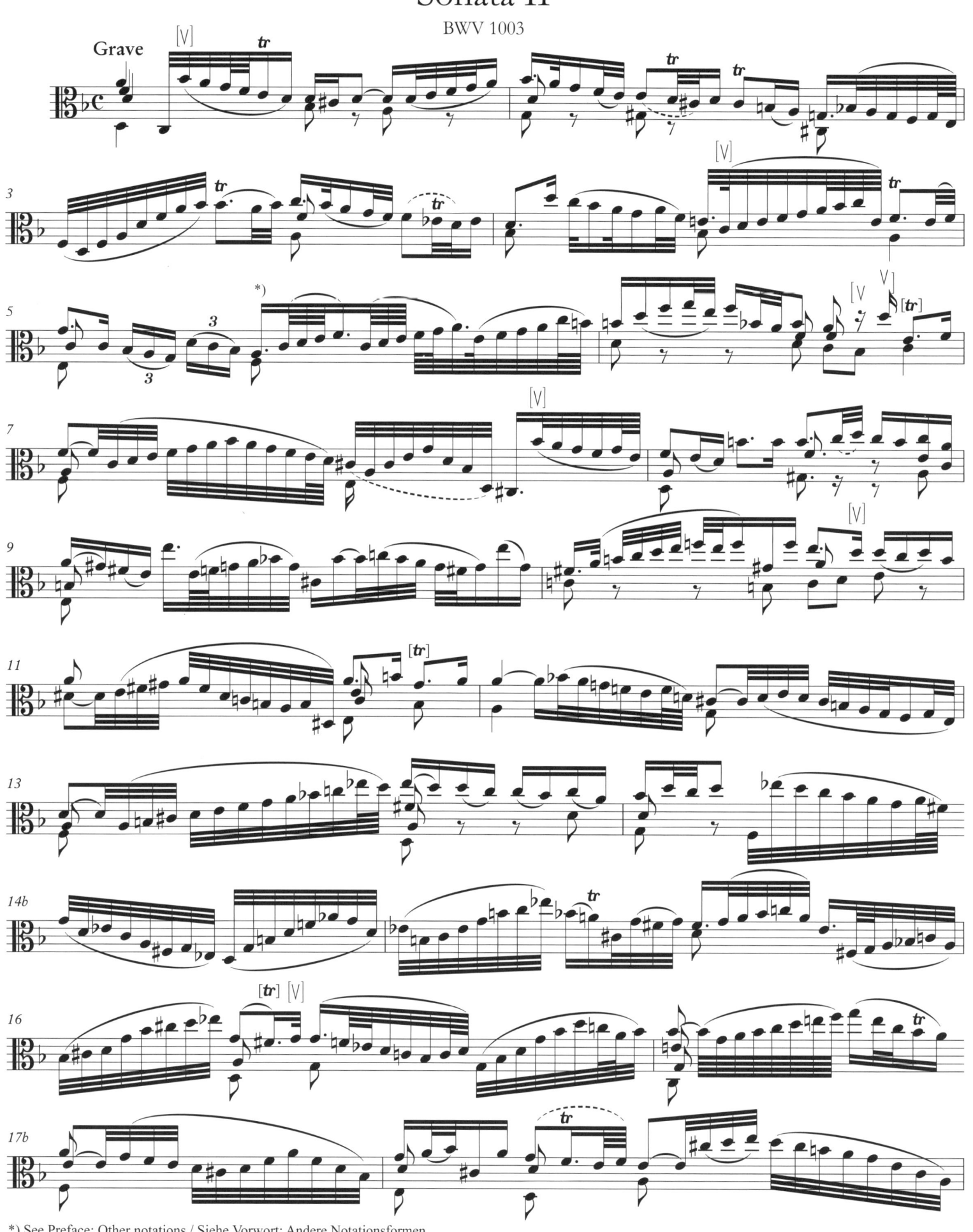

*) See Preface: Other notations / Siehe Vorwort: Andere Notationsformen

*) See Preface: Slurs and bowing: *Counterpoint* (See also Appendix Ex. 3)
Siehe Vorwort: Legatobögen und Bogenführung: *Kontrapunkt* (siehe auch Anhang, Beispiel 3)

*) See Preface: Slurs and bowing: *Counterpoint* (See also Appendix Ex. 4)
Siehe Vorwort: Legatobögen und Bogenführung, *Kontrapunkt* (siehe auch Anhang, Beispiel 4)

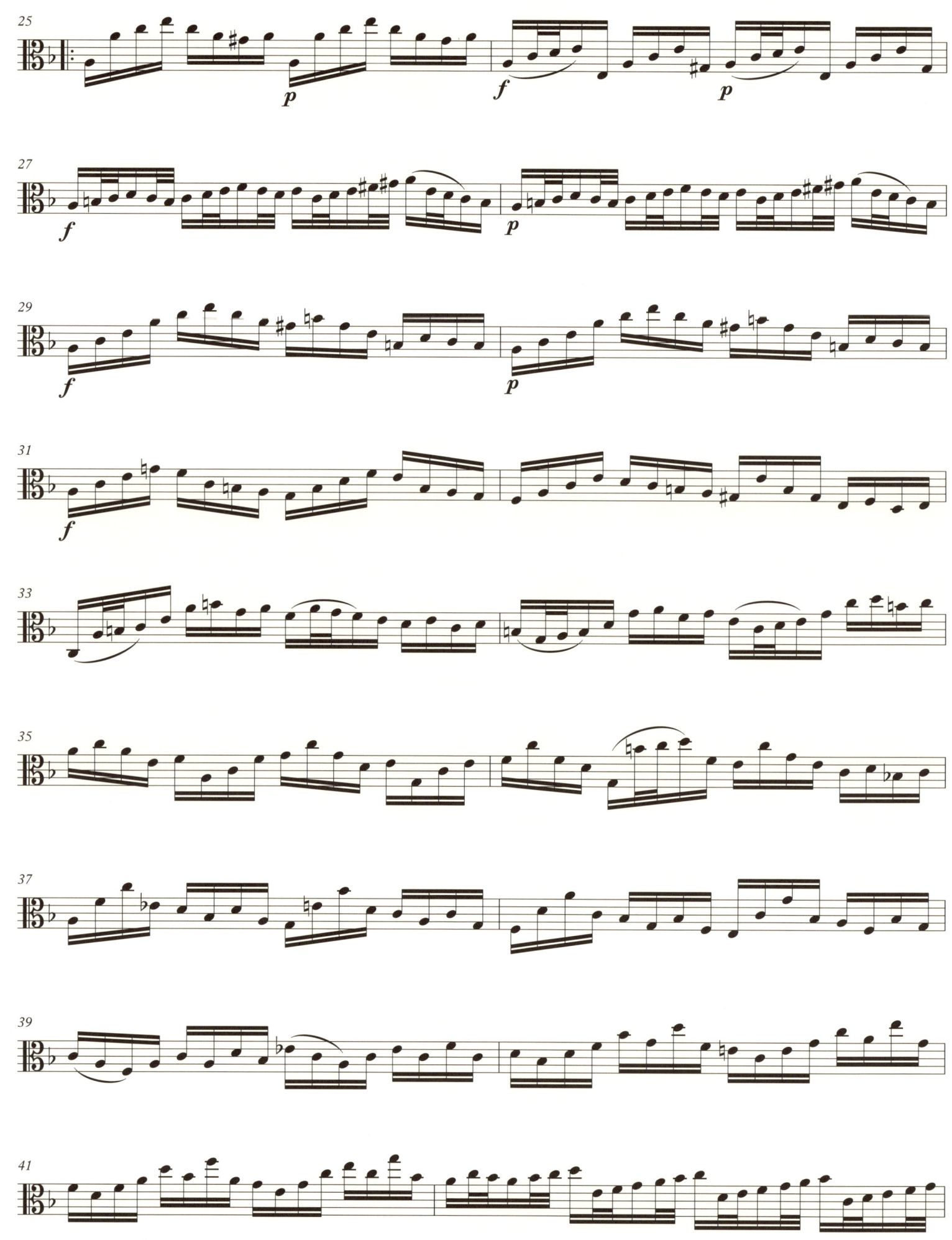

# Partita II
BWV 1004

**Allemanda**

*) See Appendix: Example 5 / Siehe Anhang: Beispiel 5

*Segue la Courante*

*) See Preface: Other notations / Siehe Vorwort: Andere Notationsformen

Sarabanda

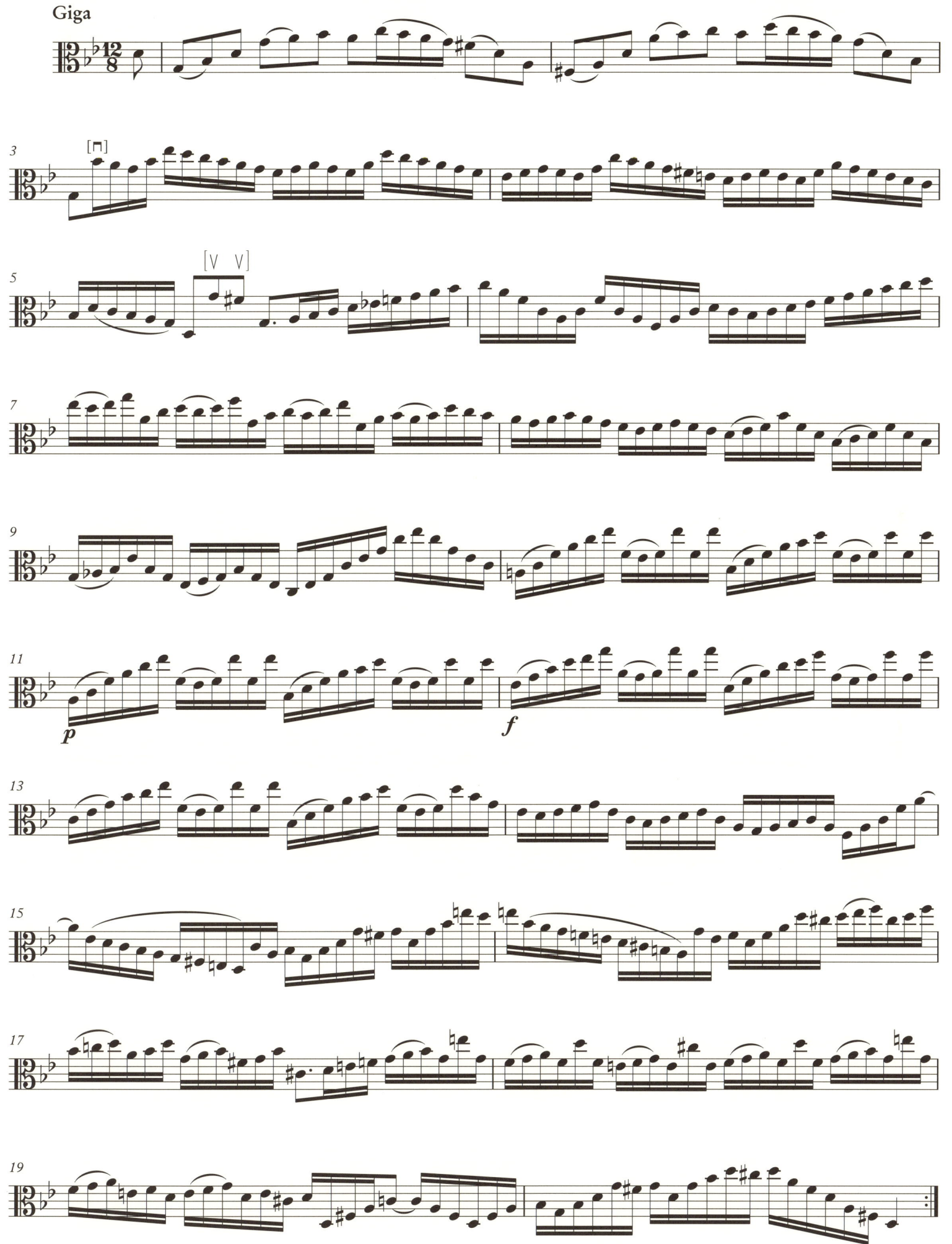

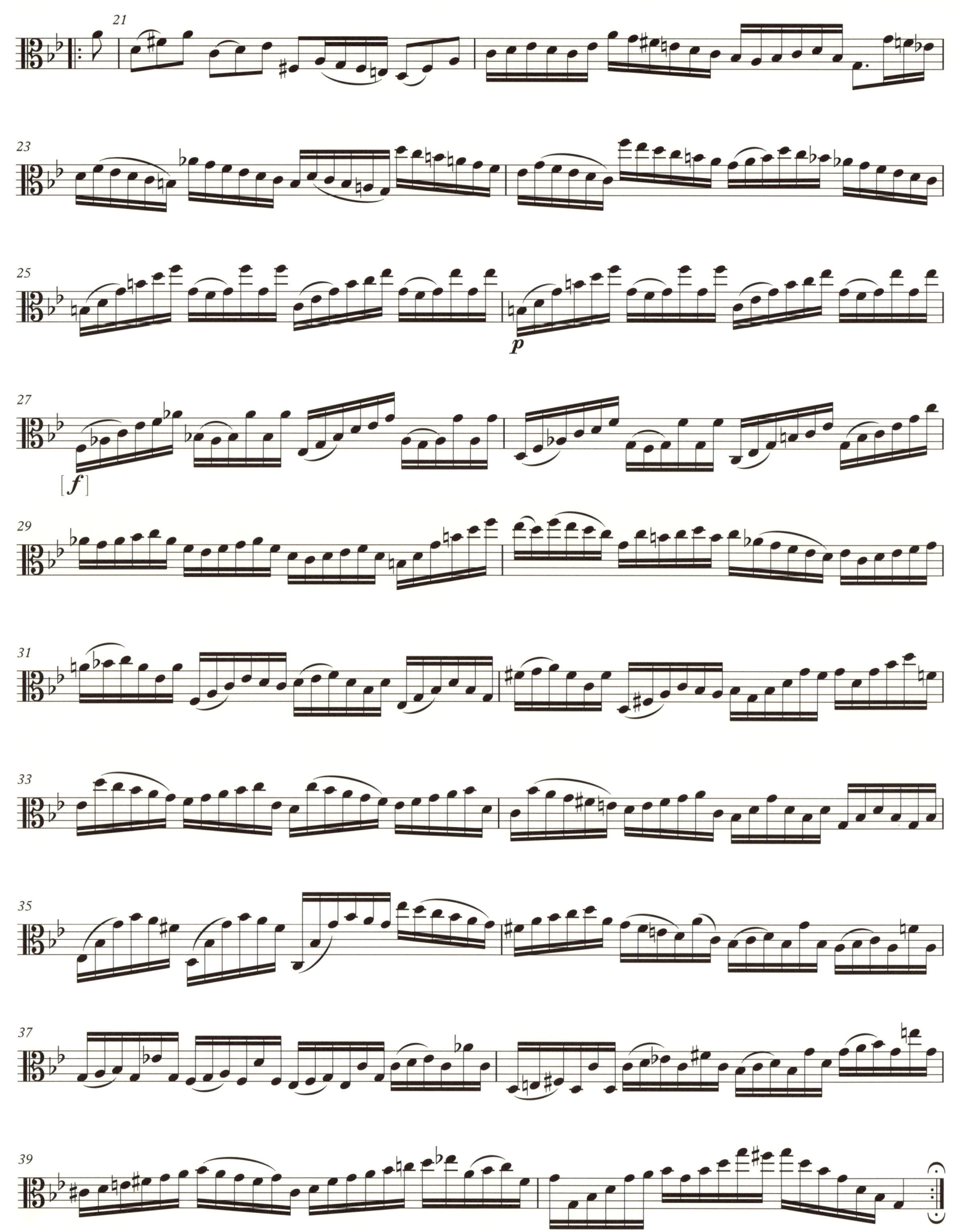

*) See Preface: Slurs and bowing *The Adagio of Sonata I* / Siehe Vorwort: Legatobögen und Bogenführung, *Sonate I, Adagio*

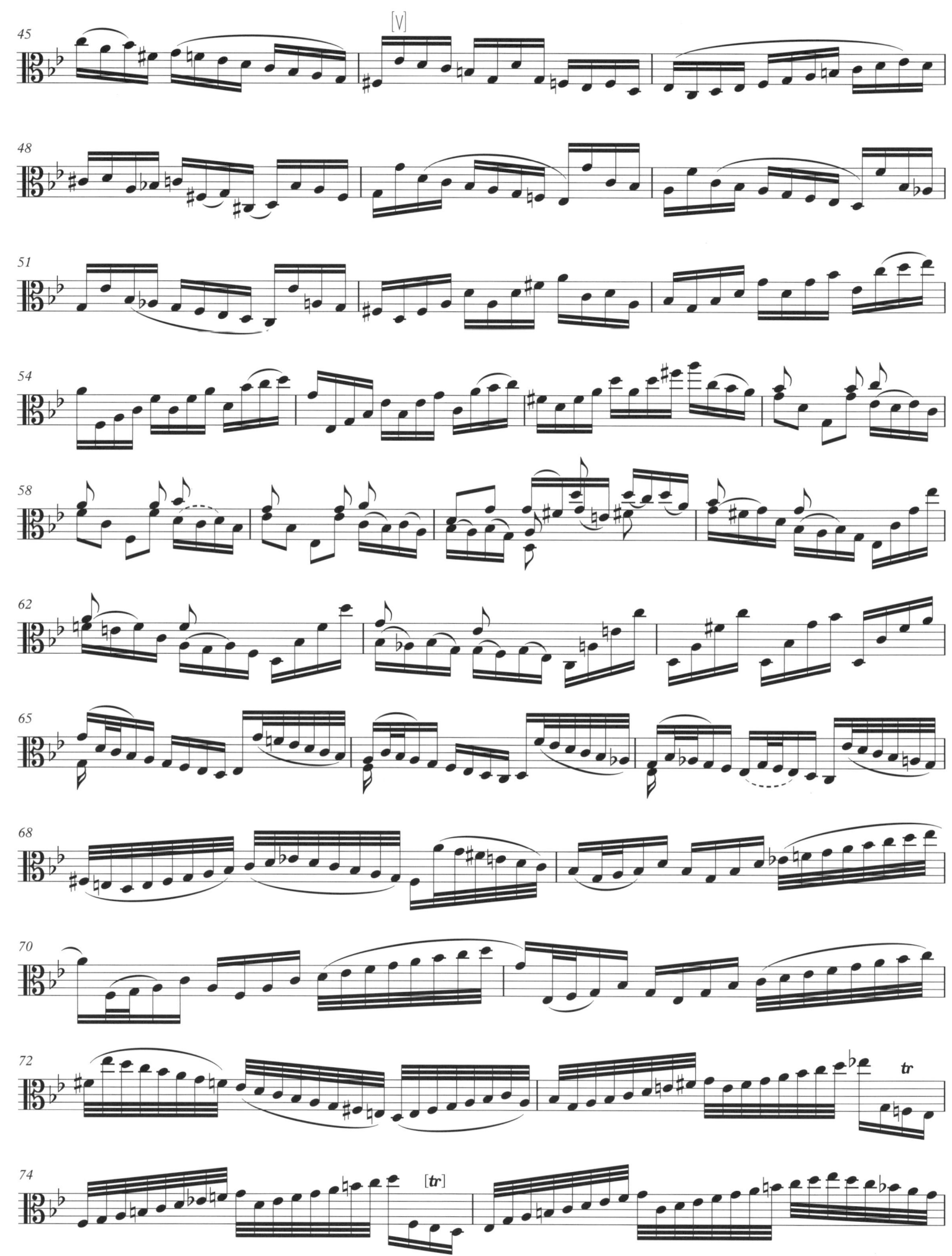

# Sonata III
BWV 1005

*) See Preface: Slurs and bowing *Counterpoint* / Siehe Vorwort: Legatobögen und Bogenführung, *Kontrapunkt*

## Fuga

*) See Preface: Slurs and bowing *General points* / Siehe Vorwort: Legatobögen und Bogenführung, *Allgemeine Hinweise*

*) See Preface: Slurs and bowing *Counterpoint* (See also Appendix Example 6)
   Siehe Vorwort: Legatobögen und Bogenführung, *Kontrapunkt* (siehe auch Anhang, Beispiel 6)

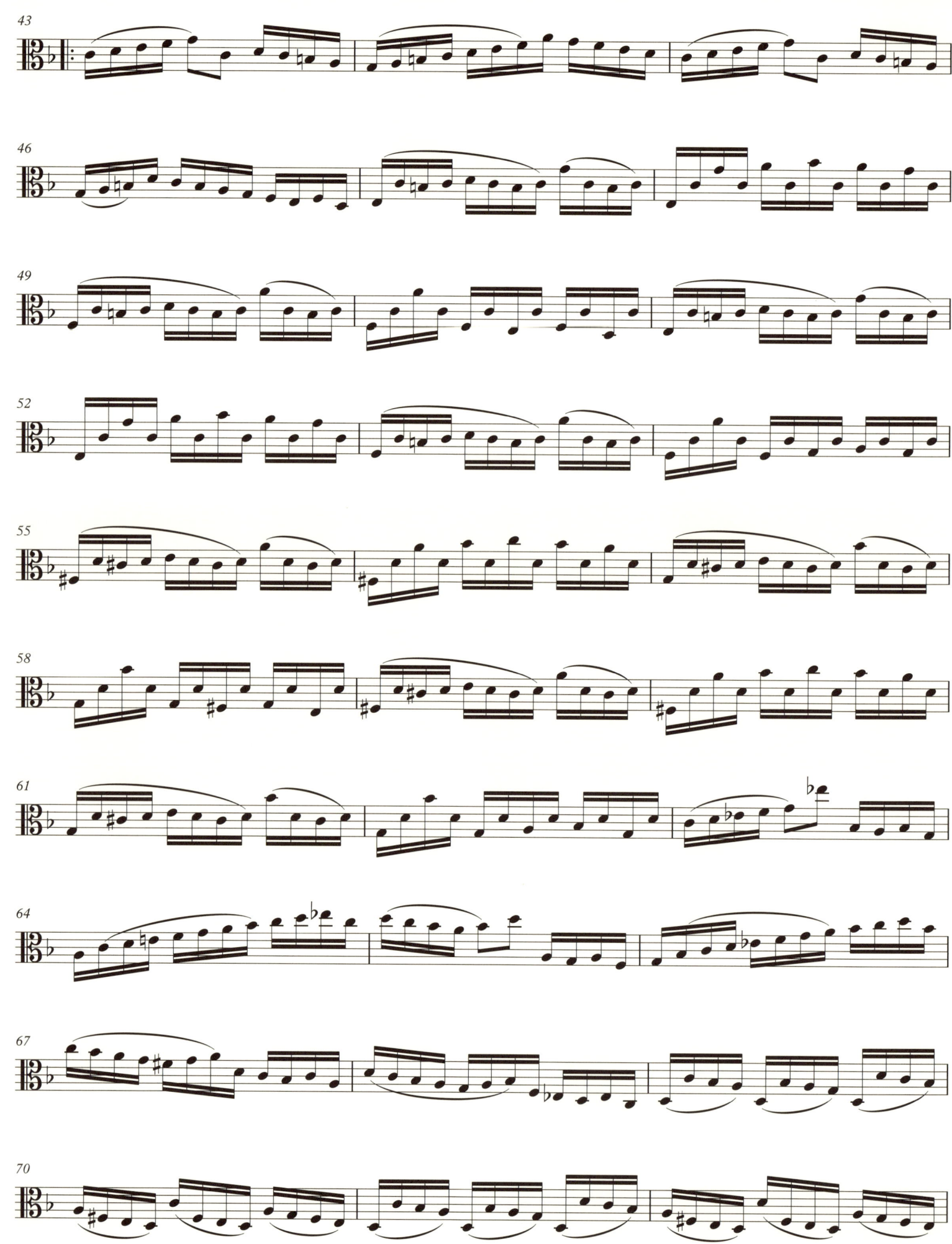

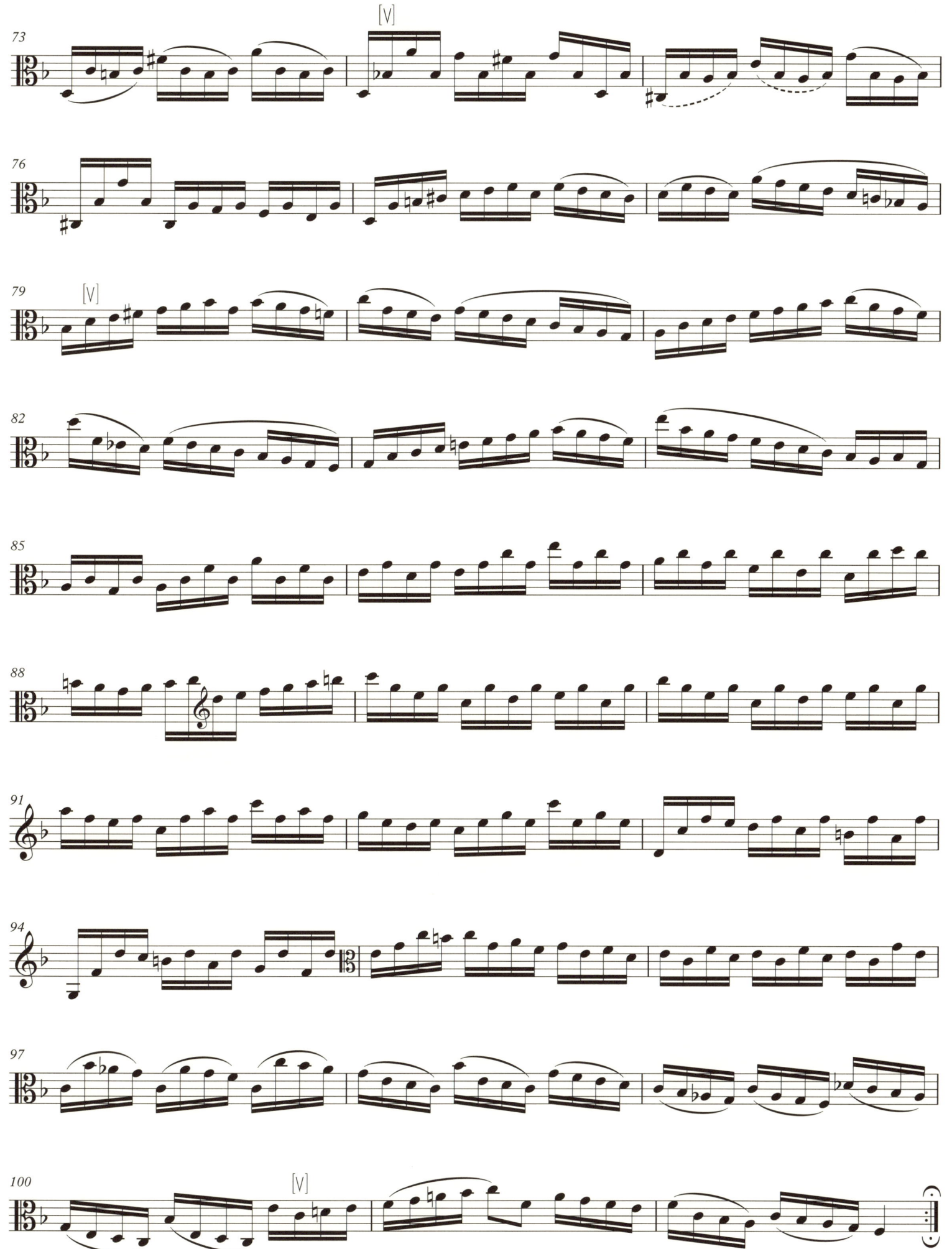

# Partita III
## BWV 1006

**Preludio**

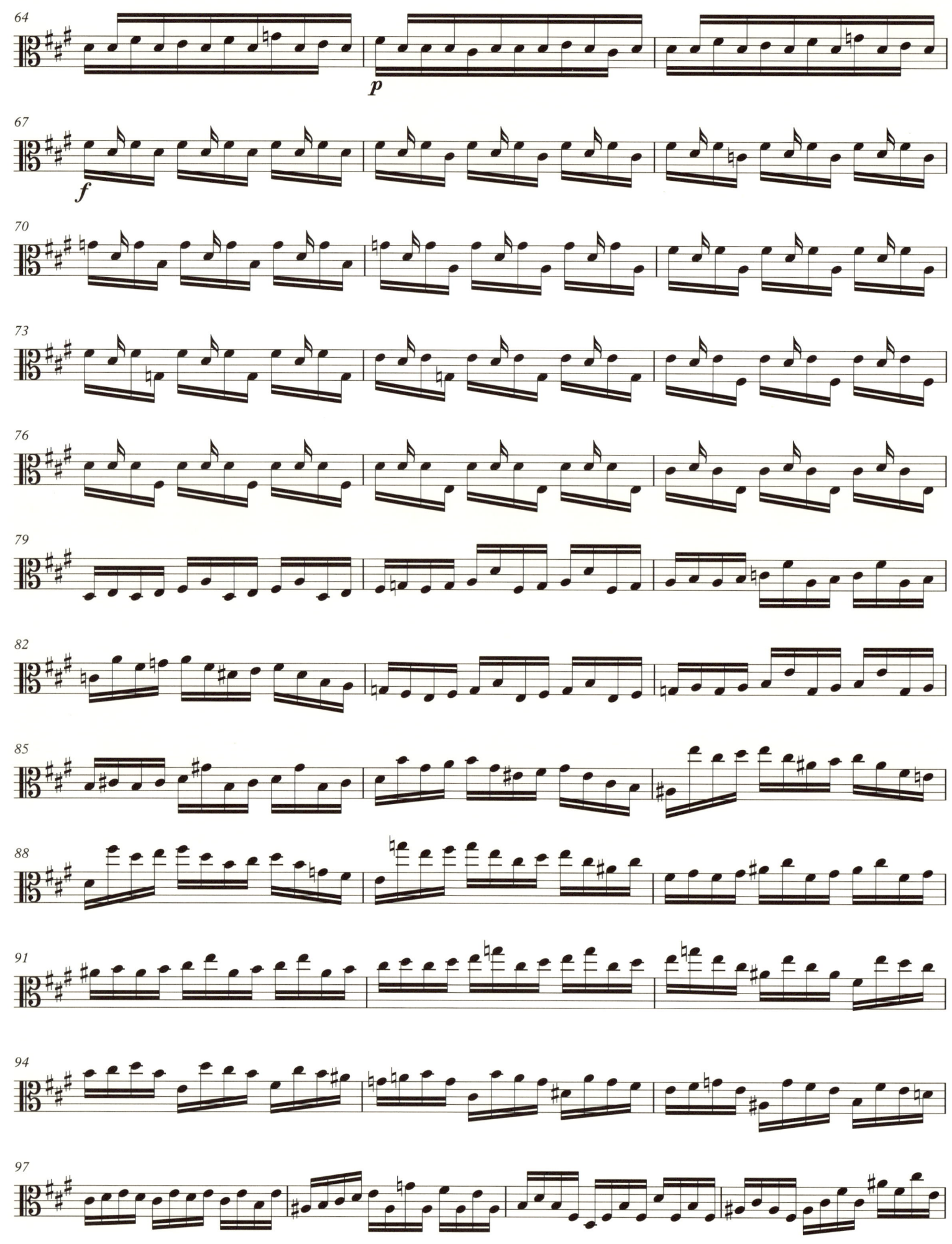

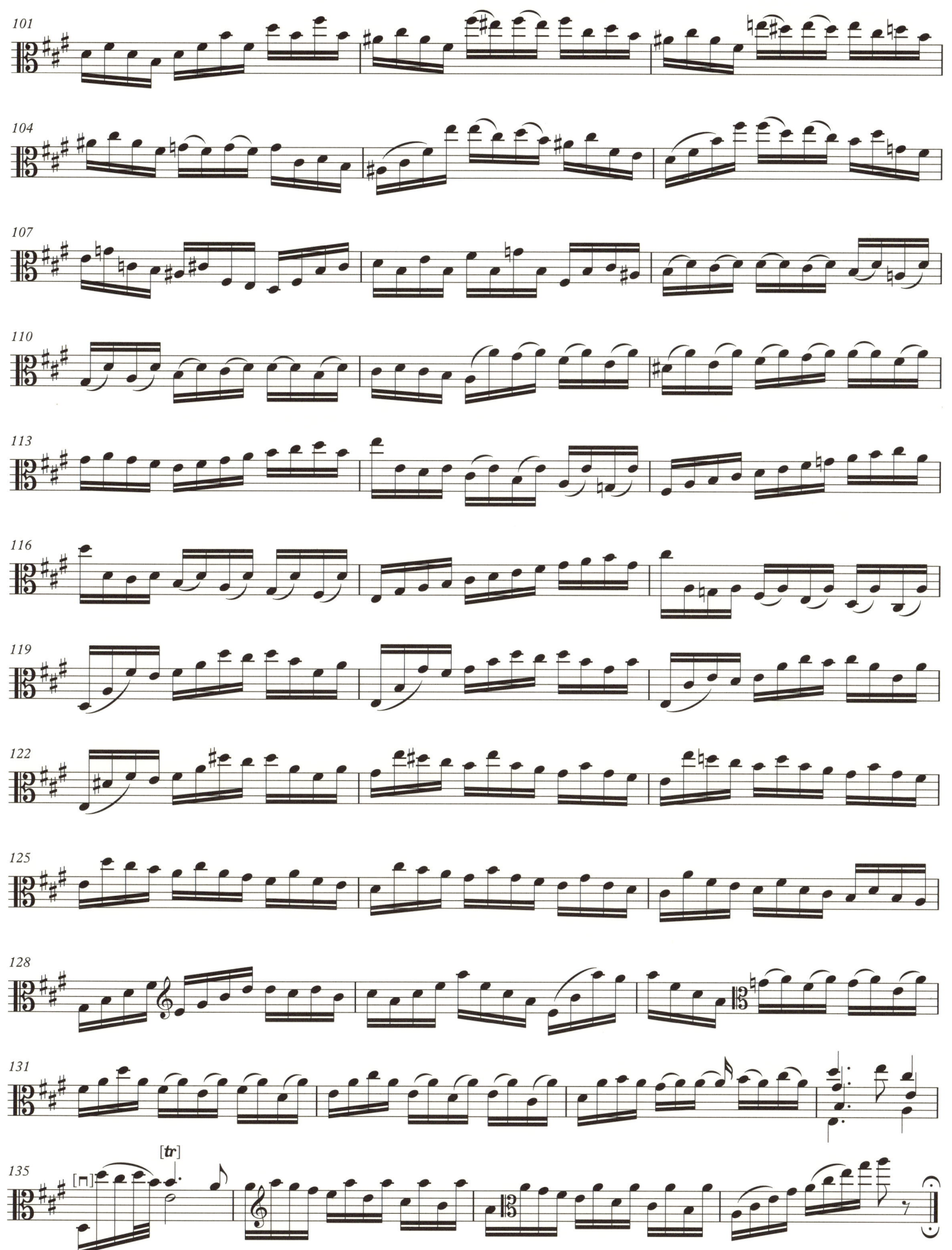

Gigue

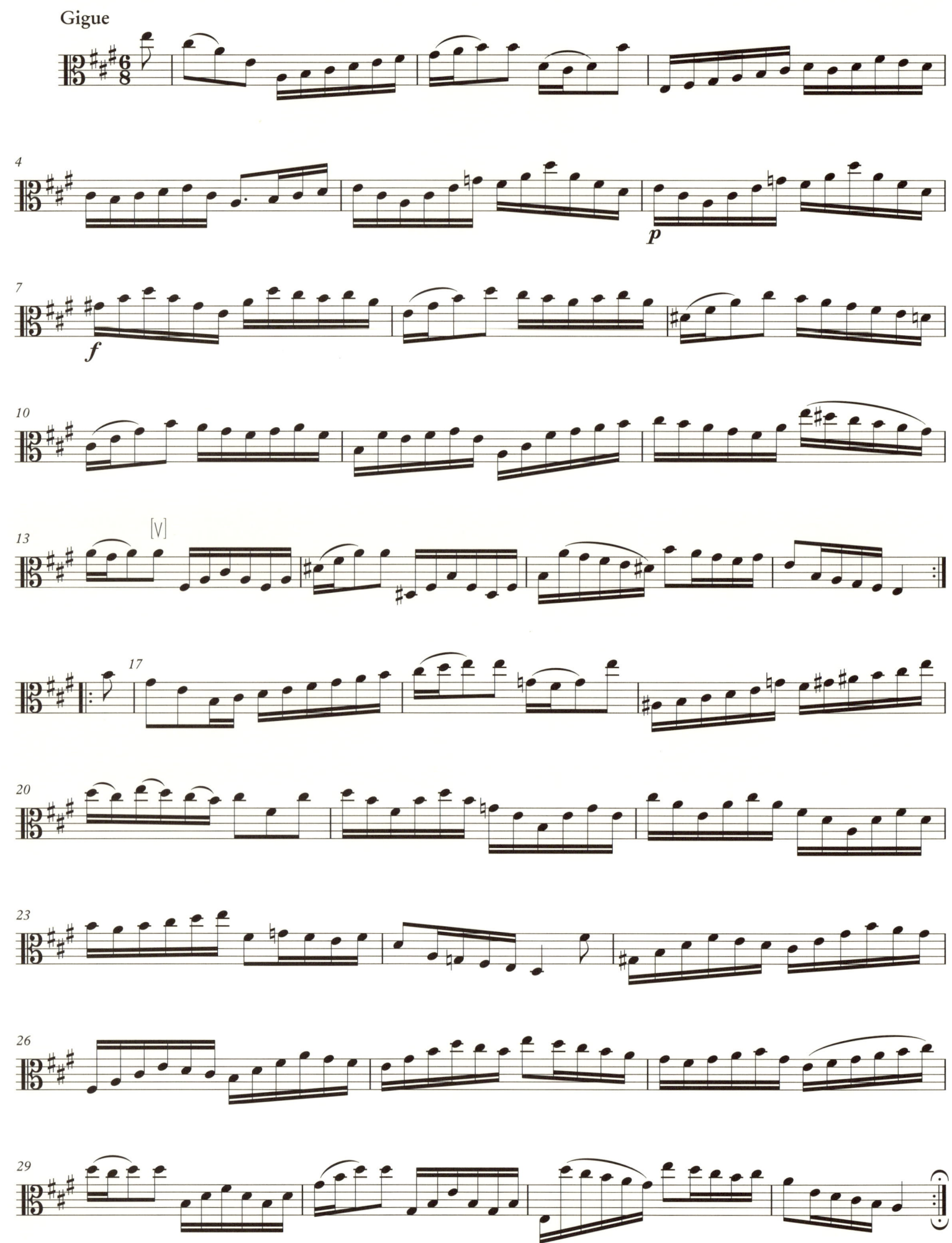

\*\*\*

# Critical Commentary

## SOURCES

**A:** by far the most important source is Bach's autograph fair copy (*D-B* Mus.ms.Bach P 967). This is one of Bach's finest calligraphic manuscripts. Bach's handwriting is highly suggestive of how he felt the music as he wrote it down so players are strongly recommended to acquire one of the many available facsimiles or view the autograph online at *Bach digital*.

**B:** of eighteen manuscript copies currently known, two are particularly close to Bach. The first was made by Anna Magdalena Bach between 1727 and 1731 (*D-B* Mus.ms.Bach P 268). This seems to have been copied from the 1720 autograph with which it shares many features. A detailed examination of its relationship to the autograph, particularly in the matter of performance indications, is in Kirsten Beißwenger's edition of the cello Suites.[1] Source B is also available online at *Bach digital*.

**C:** the other is an anonymous copy of BWV 1001–1005 made in 1721 or later (*D-B* Mus.ms.Bach P 267; it also contains BWV 1006, but in a copy made in the late 18th century by a different anonymous copyist). The copy of the first five Solos has been thought to reflect early versions since the copyist uses the flat sign (♭), rather than a natural (♮), to cancel a sharp (♯), an older manner of notation that Bach generally abandoned in 1714. On the other hand it could also be that the copyist was more familiar with this manner of notation and used it for clarity (Bach's sharps and naturals can look very similar). All in all Source C is most likely to be another copy from the 1720 autograph.[2] Since it seems to have been copied by a violinist for their own use its bowing slurs can sometimes be helpful when the autograph is ambiguous.

A further (incomplete) copy, made by Johann Peter Kellner in 1726 (*D-B* Mus.ms.Bach P 804) is compromised in various ways and has not been used for this edition. Kellner was given to making alterations on his own account. His copy is nonetheless of interest in that it may reflect an earlier version of the Solos than the 1720 autograph.[3] This source is available online at *Bach digital*.

---

[1] Beißwenger 2000, pp. 78–80.
[2] For a detailed discussion see Peter Wollny in NBA*rev*/3, pp. 214–15; for an opposing view see Fanselau 2013, pp. 224–8.
[3] See Stinson 1990, Chapter III; also Szabó 2015.

## INDIVIDUAL REMARKS

Pitches are always referred to as the pitches in the transcribed viola version, even in reference to the manuscript sources.
Helmholtz system – c (tenor)  c′ (middle)  c″ (treble)  c‴ (in alt)

### Sonata I   C minor   BWV 1001

#### Adagio

**b1**
2$^{nd}$ beat slur: C (see Preface: Slurs and Bowing *The Adagio of Sonata I*) A nn2–8 B nn2–7

3$^{rd}$ beat slur: editorially added to conform with similar appoggiaturas in bb4, 8, 21 (see Preface: Slurs and Bowing *The Adagio of Sonata I*)

**b2**
slur nn3–11: editorially amended in order to arrive on a down-bow on 3$^{rd}$ beat (see Preface: Slurs and Bowing *The Adagio of Sonata I*) AB nn2–11; C nn1–11

**b3**
3$^{rd}$ beat flat sign in lower voice: C and to conform with analogous b16 (AB no flat sign but as the other three occurrences in b3 of the pitch a flat do have the flat sign, this is assumed by the present edition to be an oversight)

3$^{rd}$ beat slur: editorial interpretation (see Preface: Slurs and Bowing *The Adagio of Sonata I*) and in order to arrive on a down-bow on b4 (ABC nn3–8)

4$^{th}$ beat 128$^{th}$ nn11,12: C (AB 64$^{th}$ notes)

**b4**
3$^{rd}$ beat slur: editorial interpretation (see Preface: Slurs and Bowing *The Adagio of Sonata I* - Bach's writing habits) ABC nn2–4

**b5**
3$^{rd}$ beat slur: editorial interpretation (Preface: Slurs and Bowing *The Adagio of Sonata I* - Bach's writing habits) ABC nn2–3

**b6**
n1 upper voice: flat sign editorially added to conform with upbeat (ABC no flat sign)

**b16**
4$^{th}$ beat slur: C (AB nn 2–7)

**b17**
3$^{rd}$ beat slur: C (see Preface: Slurs and Bowing *The Adagio of Sonata I* - Bach's writing habits) AB nn2–4

#### Fuga

**b12**
slur nn1–3: editorial interpretation (see Preface: Slurs and Bowing *The Adagio of Sonata I* - Bach's writing habits) AB nn2–3; C no slur

**b57**
4$^{th}$ beat slur: editorial interpretation (see Preface: Slurs and Bowing *The Adagio of Sonata I* - Bach's writing habits) A nn3–4; B four sixteenth notes with slur nn2–3; C no slur

**b83**
slur nn2–3: editorially added to conform with 3$^{rd}$ beat of bar

### Siciliana

b7

3rd beat slur: editorially added to conform with b5 nn1–2 and similar places

b14

slur nn1–2: C and to conform with nn1–2, 7–8, 9–10 etc.

slur nn3–4: editorially added to conform with nn1–2

### Partita I   E minor   BWV 1002

### Allemanda

bb7, 23

4th beat slur: editorially amended (see Preface: Slurs and Bowing *General points*) AB nn1–2; C no slur

b21

4th beat slur nn1–3: BC (A no slur)

### Sonata II   D minor   BWV 1003

### Grave

b2

2nd beat slur: editorially amended (see Preface: Slurs and Bowing *General points*) ABC nn1–2

b3

4th beat slur: editorially amended (as in b2 - see Preface: Slurs and Bowing *General points*) ABC nn1–2

b7

3rd beat slur: editorial interpretation (see Preface: Slurs and Bowing *The Adagio of Sonata I* - Bach's writing habits) ABC nn2–8

b22

1st and 2nd beats: editorially amended for ease of execution (ABC nn1–16)

### Fuga

b183

n6: AB (C *d′* instead of *c′*)

b263

slur nn2–4: B and to conform with bb265, 267 (A nn1–3; C no slur)

### Partita II   G minor   BWV 1004

### Gigue

b27

*f*: editorially added to conform with analogous b12

### Ciaccona

bb4, 5, 252, 253

slurs: editorial interpretation (see Preface: Slurs and Bowing *The Adagio of Sonata I* - Bach's writing habits) ABC nn2–4 except C b4 where the slur is nn1–4

### Sonata III   F major   BWV 1005

### Largo

b7

slur: editorially added to conform with b2 nn1–3

### Allegro assai

b75

slur: editorially amended to conform with bb24, 26, 73 (ABC nn1–8)

# Appendix

Examples with suggestions for performance mentioned in the **Preface**.

Notes in brackets indicate practical editorial suggestions for possible adjustments to note lengths and are only approximate.

Example 1:   Sonata I   C minor BWV1001   Fuga   bb15–18

Example 2:   Sonata I   C minor BWV1001   Fuga   bb35–36

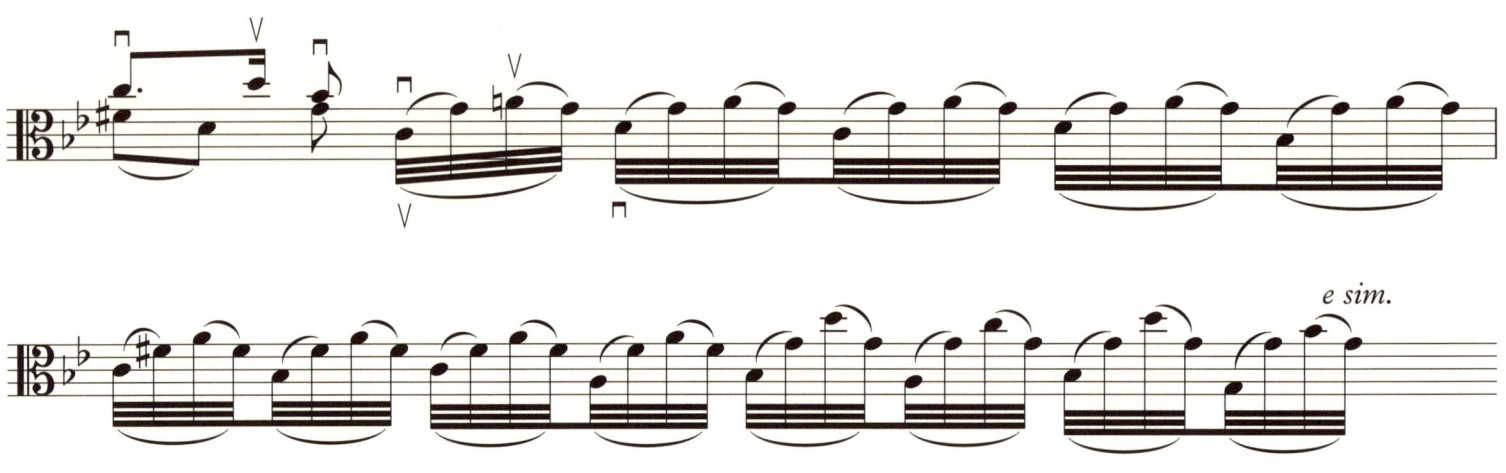

Example 3:   Sonata II   D minor   BWV1003   Fuga   bb128–130

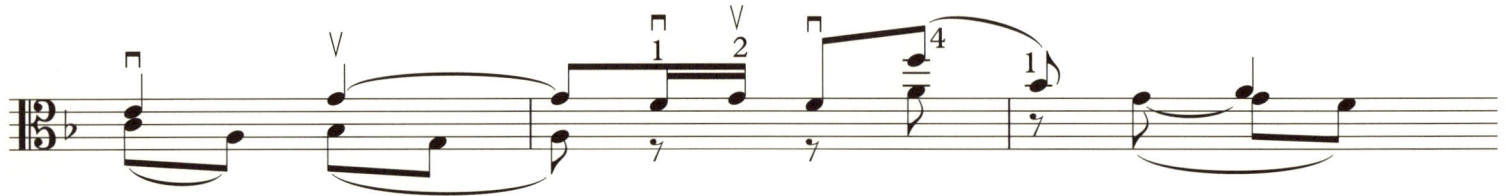

Example 4: Sonata II   D minor   BWV1003   Andante   bb1–4

Example 5: Partita II   G minor   BWV1004   Allemanda   bb9–10

Example 6: Sonata III   F major   BWV1005   Fuga bb115-121

Example 7: Partita III   A major   BWV1006   Loure   bb1–4 with ornaments from BWV1006a (See Preface: Mixed style)

**Example 8:** Bach's Table of Ornaments (1720)

*Explication* unterschiedlicher Zeichen, so gewisse *manieren* artig zu spielen, andeuten.
Explanation of various signs, showing how to play certain ornaments neatly.

# References

*Abbreviations*

| | |
|---|---|
| D-B | Staatsbibliothek zu Berlin, Preußischer Kulturbesitz, Musikabteilung mit Mendessohn-Archiv |
| NBA V/10 | *Johann Sebastian Bach. Neue Ausgabe sämtlicher Werke, Serie V. Band 10: Einzeln überlieferte Klavierwerke II und Kompositionen für Lauteninstrumente*, ed. H. Eichberg and T. Kohlhase (Kassel: Bärenreiter, 1976) |
| NBA VI/1 | *Johann Sebastian Bach. Neue Ausgabe sämtlicher Werke, Serie VI. Band 1: Werke für Violine*, ed. G. Haußwald and R. Gerber (Kassel: Bärenreiter, 1958) |
| NBArev/3 | *Johann Sebastian Bach. Neue Ausgabe sämtlicher Werke, Revidierte Edition. Band 3: Kammermusik mit Violine*, ed. P. Wollny (Kassel: Bärenreiter, 2014) |
| NBR | *The New Bach Reader*, ed. H. T. David and A. Mendel, revised C. Wolff (New York: Norton, 1998) |

*Editions and Literature*

Beißwenger, K. (ed.). *Johann Sebastian Bach. Six Suites for Violoncello Solo* (Wiesbaden: Breitkopf & Härtel, 2000)

Boyden, D. *The History of Violin Playing from its Origins to 1761* (London: Oxford University Press, 1965)

Couperin, F. *L'Art de toucher le clavecin* (Paris, 2/1717)

Emery, W. *Bach's Ornaments* (Sevenoaks: Novello, 1953)

Fanselau, C. 'Sei Solo â Violino senza Basso accompagnato BWV 1001–1006', *Das Bach-Handbuch. Band 5/2: Bachs Orchester- und Kammermusik*, ed. S. Rampe and D. Sackmann (Laaber: Laaber, 2013), pp. 211–52

Joachim, J. and Moser, A. (eds). *Johann Sebastian Bach. Sonaten und Partiten für Violine allein* (Berlin: Bote & Bock, 1908)

Klotz, H. *Die Ornamentik der Klavier- und Orgelwerke von Johann Sebastian Bach* (Kassel: Bärenreiter, 1984)

Kolneder, W. *Georg Muffat zur Aufführungspraxis* (Baden-Baden: Verlag Valentin Koerner, 2/1990)

Le Blanc, H. *Defense de la basse de viole contre les entreprises du violon et les prétentions du violoncel* (Amsterdam, 1740)

Ledbetter, D. *Unaccompanied Bach : Performing the Solo Works* (New Haven, CT: Yale University Press, 2009)

Lester, J. *Bach's Works for Solo Violin: Style, Structure, Performance* (New York: Oxford University Press, 1999)

Moens-Haenen, G. 'Zur Frage der Wellenlinien in der Musik Johann Sebastian Bachs', *Archiv für Musikwissenschaft* xli/3 (1984), pp. 176–86

— *Das Vibrato in der Musik des Barock* (Graz: Akademische Druck- und Verlagsanstalt, 1988)

Mozart, L. *Versuch einer gründlichen Violinschule* (Augsburg, 1756); English trans. E. Knocker, *A Treatise on the Fundamental Principles of Violin Playing* (Oxford: Oxford University Press, 3/1985); trad. française partielle V. Roeser, *Méthode de violon* (Paris, 1770) (fac-similé Paris: Zurfluh, 1993)

Muffat, G. *Florilegium secundum* (Passau, 1698); English trans. Wilson 2001, pp. 28–65; synoptic ed. Kolneder 1990, pp. 39–99

Quantz, J. J. *Versuch einer Anweisung die Flöte traversiere zu spielen* (Berlin, 1752); English trans. E.R. Reilly, *On Playing the Flute* (London: Faber and Faber, 2/1985); version française, *Essai d'une méthode pour apprendre à jouer de la flûte traversière* (fac-similé Paris: Zurfluh, 1975)

Schröder, J. *Bach's Solo Violin Works: A Performer's Guide* (New Haven, CT: Yale University Press, 2007)

Stinson, R. *The Bach Manuscripts of Johann Peter Kellner and his Circle* (Durham, NC: Duke University Press, 1990)

Szabó, Z. 'Remaining silhouettes of lost Bach manuscripts? Re-evaluating J. P. Kellner's copy of J. S. Bach's solo string compositions', *Understanding Bach* 10 (2015), pp. 71–83

Wilson, D. K. *Georg Muffat on Performance Practice* (Bloomington, IN: Indiana University Press, 2001)